Speaking
It's NOT Worse Than Death

Kaylene Ledgar

First published by Ultimate World Publishing 2019
Copyright © 2019 Kaylene Ledgar

ISBN

Paperback - 978-1-925884-48-7
Ebook - 978-1-925884-49-4

Kaylene Ledgar has asserted her right under the Copyright, Designs and Patents Act 1988 to be identified as the author of this work. The information in this book is based on the author's experiences and opinions. The publisher specifically disclaims responsibility for any adverse consequences, which may result from use of the information contained herein. Permission to use information has been sought by the author. Any breaches will be rectified in further editions of the book.

All rights reserved. No part of this publication may be reproduced, stored in or introduced into a retrieval system, or transmitted in any form, or by any means (electronic, mechanical, photocopying, recording or otherwise) without the prior written permission of the author. Any person who does any unauthorised act in relation to this publication may be liable to criminal prosecution and civil claims for damages. Enquiries should be made through the publisher.

Cover design: Ultimate World Publishing
Layout and typesetting: Ultimate World Publishing
Editor: James Salmon

Ultimate World Publishing
Diamond Creek,
Victoria Australia 3089
www.writeabook.com.au

What People Are Saying

"Professional, eloquent and articulate, Kaylene is a top speaker and presenter, who enthralls audiences with her style.

Kaylene's coaching style is transformational and I would recommend her to all who want to become the best version of themselves."

David A Hughes,
Speaker and Facilitator, I Can Do Words

"Kaylene is a thoroughly knowledgeable, yet humble, educator with a wealth of experience which she willingly imparts to fledgling public speakers.

Kaylene brings years of experience in leadership and public speaking skills. She has travelled widely to attend the Toastmaster International World Championships of Public Speaking and harnesses knowledge she has gleaned from world class masters in this art form.

Kaylene has the incredible and rare skill of empathising with every speaker at whatever stage of their development. Kaylene is then able to provide compelling and challenging feedback to enable them to boldly take their next steps towards achieving their dreams."

Arnjali Amarasingham,
Senior Government Lawyer, Department of Human Services

"Kaylene is a sincere leader who leads her team from the front. She is an excellent authentic communicator and a great listener. As a mentor and coach, she brings a wealth of knowledge and experience from her time as a past leader of an international non-profit education organisation and her role in the Australian Public Service. As a speaker and trainer, she connects with the audience through her conversational style.

Kaylene inspires future leaders and speakers."

Alicia Curtis,
Senior Broker, Bruce Chiene Insurance Brokers

"Kaylene is an authentic person. Her authenticity shines through in everything she does, whether that is giving a speech or in a coaching session. Kaylene makes people comfortable with her engaging, compassionate and authentic communication style. Kaylene has lived the fear of public speaking and has become a fantastic and generous speaker."

Rebecca Plush DTM,
District 70 Director 2016-2017, Toastmasters International

"I met Kaylene through Toastmasters and I was very quickly inspired by not only her public speaking skills, but also her dedication and determination to help others. She became my mentor and I have learnt so much from her. She has continued to encourage and challenge me which has led to me building my confidence and capabilities.

Kaylene has been a great mentor and inspiration in my life and I will be forever grateful for all that I have learned from her."

Taryn Wainman,
Immediate Past President, Toastmaster Club District 69

"I have been so impressed by Kaylene's public speaking skills every time I have heard her talk in front of the audience. Her presentations are always engaging, interesting, clearly articulated and easy to follow. Her impromptu speech is always my personal favourite, delivered with genuineness, wits, confidence and coherence.

I was fortunate enough to have Kaylene coaching me over a period of time, during which she tailored her approach to my needs and focusing areas. The coaching sessions she provided me were comprehensive, educational and motivational, filled with lots of timely constructive feedback and I could feel almost immediate improvement on my speech construction and delivery. The tips, suggestions, exercises and feedback that she offered me are useful and effective, and I can see positive results derived since then on my personal skills, social interactions and career development.

I highly recommend Kaylene and her mentoring/coaching/training work to anyone who's keen on improving communication skills. Regardless of your current level of proficiency, I guarantee you will learn, improve, and be inspired and enlightened from Kaylene on this value-adding development journey.

And for all the amazing and invaluable techniques, confidence, advices and exemplary performances that she has shown, I can't thank her enough. Thank you Kaylene for a wonderful learning experience!"

Queenie Wei,
Financial Analyst, Treasury

"Kaylene is a real inspiration and support. She was amazing help when I first joined Toastmasters to overcome my fear of public speaking. I would highly recommend her as a coach. I couldn't have done it without you. I now have the confidence to public speak. Thank you!"

Sara Kennedy,
Vice President Membership, Canberra Gourmet Toastmasters Club

I am in a unique position in terms of providing a testimonial for Kaylene and her public speaking journey. I was there at the start when she attended her first Toastmasters Speechcraft Course in 2003. When I think of Kaylene and her journey, it reminds me of the lyric "from crayons to perfume" from the song "To Sir with Love". I knew her from the time where just having to say her name in front of an audience brought about extreme feelings of fear and nervousness, to a time where she jumps at the opportunity to give an impromptu speech in front of an audience of 100's.

Through knowing her, I know of a person who listens, can provide valuable feedback and, most importantly, is patient. If you require someone to support you and coach you on your journey, then Kaylene is the person for you.

Timothy Reed,
Solutions Architect, Department of Human Services

Kaylene displays a great understanding of the underlying principles of the impact of constructive feedback for a speaker. She puts this understanding to work when coaching speakers within Toastmasters. She further displayed this by winning the Toastmasters District 70 Evaluation Speech contest, a contest which is designed to provide constructive respectful feedback to a target speaker.

Kaylene has displayed great leadership within the organisation, becoming the District 70 Governor in 2011-2012. This all means Kaylene knows what it takes for a speaker to stand on the stage and present an inspirational presentation.

Kaylene is a source of inspiration.

John Jennings DTM,
District 70 Director 2018-2019, Toastmasters International

Kaylene has been my mentor in Toastmasters since I joined over 10 years ago. She is always approachable, and her advice is invaluable. What I appreciate about Kaylene is her encouragement of others.

Kaylene has always given outstanding speech evaluations, where she provides feedback on someone else's presentation. Not only does she provide excellent and actionable advice to the speaker, but she also frames the evaluations such that everyone present receives pertinent insights into how they can also improve their own speeches.

Kaylene is simply wired to encourage and support others to reach their potential.

Andrew Main,
President Namadgi Toastmasters Club

Kaylene is a great motivator and teacher ... her high energy and enthusiasm is contagious.

Scott Johnson,
Speaker, Communication Coach and Trainer, Speaker Forum

I recall a speech by Kaylene about the benefits of improving public speaking and how it changed her life, and was fortunate to have the opportunity to be coached by Kaylene. The coaching by Kaylene has given me the confidence to stand in front of an audience and tell a story in an engaging manner, without the um's and ah's.

Kathryn Walters,
Assistant Director, Department of Human Services

Kaylene's been a very good mentor and coach. Kaylene literally makes the dumb speak - I became a better public speaker through the mentoring and coaching skills of Kaylene.

Amadu Barrie,
ICT System Analyst, Department of Human Services

Speaking It's NOT Worse Than Death

Dedication

To my first speaking mentor, Dawn Summers,
who believed I could, when all I saw was fear.

To my brother David, for keeping me grounded.

To my brother John, for helping me unlock my purpose.

To my mum Lavinia, for encouraging me to follow my dreams.

To my dad David, for inspiring me to live my life with no regrets.

Speaking It's NOT Worse Than Death

Contents

What People Are Saying iii
Dedication ix
Contents xi
Introduction 1
Self-assessment: It's All About You 5
Chapter 1: Fear Busting 11
Chapter 2: Getting Started 25
Chapter 3: The Right Package 37
Chapter 4: Unlock Your Story 51
Chapter 5: To Q & A or Not 67
Chapter 6: The Bookends Matter 81
Chapter 7: Using Your Voice 91
Chapter 8: Make a Move 101
Chapter 9: Selecting Your Accessories 111
Chapter 10: Let's Get Social 127
Chapter 11: Bringing It All Together 135
Chapter 12: What Next? 145
Bonus Chapter: From The Heart With Tears 157
Afterword 175
About the Author 177
Acknowledgements 179
FREE Resources 181

Speaking It's NOT Worse Than Death

Introduction

*It is often said that
the fear of public speaking ranks higher than death.
I disagree, public speaking is not worse than death.
You can survive a speech. You can't survive death.*
KAYLENE LEDGAR

◆ ◆ ◆

Congratulations on deciding to face your fear. You are about to embark on your own personal journey of discovery that will take you to unexpected and wonderful places. When you eliminate your fear of speaking, doors will open that you never imagined. Instead of turning and running, you will walk through the door with confidence, ready to face the new adventure, the new opportunity and the chance to continue learning.

As you face your fear and develop your skills as a speaker, there may be times when you feel overwhelmed. If you do feel overwhelmed at any point, I encourage you to hang in there, take a deep breath and keep going. Sometimes to reach the best view, you have to navigate a challenging path.

The fear of public speaking used to consume me. Now speaking excites me.

At the height of my fear of speaking, I struggled to speak in front of two people or more. My boss used to say it was like pulling teeth, to get me to speak in team meetings. The thought of having to speak in front of the team horrified me. If I was asked to speak, I would be overcome with a sick feeling in my tummy and my knees would shake uncontrollably under the table. I hated speaking and did all I could to avoid it.

Then, I was faced with a dilemma. I wanted to advance in my career and desperately wanted to win a promotion, however, to win the promotion, I had to face my fear of speaking in front of a two-person interview panel.

The need for me to win the promotion far outweighed my fear. That was the first step for me to overcome my fear of public speaking. I decided to take action and signed up for an eight-week Speechcraft Course run by a local Toastmasters Club. I was terrified of speaking in front of strangers. In any other course, I would have listened, observed and never said a word however this was a public speaking course and that meant I had to speak. Week by week, I started to develop my skills as a speaker, learning how to structure a speech and how to manage my nerves. Slowly I started to gain some confidence. At the end of the course I was still nervous to speak in front of groups and apprehensive about the interview. I used my new found speaking skills and knowledge to prepare for the interview. I actually practiced answering questions. I used the deep breathing technique I had learnt, to calm my nerves before I went in for the interview. I didn't just survive the interview; I won the promotion.

I took action because I valued winning the promotion more than my fear. I made a conscious decision to not let my fear override my career opportunities. Imagine what you could do if you de-valued your fear.

My life since then has been one of professional development and self-realisation. I continue to be amazed by the value that is gained when investing in continued learning. There are always the expected benefits – like from this book you will gain tips on how to overcome your fear of speaking, you will unlock keys to developing a powerful speech and you will appreciate that your speech is more than just words. The unexpected benefits are the gems, the icing on the cake. As you navigate through this book and building your speech, look for how you can use what you are learning in your everyday life. I personally have found the clarity gained from speech preparation and planning helps me clearly define my goals.

I believe that when our actions match our values, we unlock our true path. I am passionate about supporting people to overcome their fear of speaking, to develop their skills as a speaker and realise their potential. This is what has driven me to write this book.

In this book, I have packaged the keys that have helped me to bust my fear of speaking along with the tools I use as a speaker and a speaking coach. As you unlock the keys in this book, one by one, your confidence will grow and your fear of speaking will be reduced.

To make the most out of this book, follow the activities for each chapter in the order they are provided, starting with the self-assessment. By doing this you will craft a speech that will be clear and purposeful, you will deliver the speech with style and become a more confident speaker.

Visit www.kayleneledgar.com.au/speechprepwb to download your FREE copy of:

- Speaking, It's NOT Worse Than Death workbook.

As I write this book, the loss of my dad earlier this year is still very raw. The memory of having to prepare and deliver the eulogy at his celebration of life has inspired me to provide a bonus chapter. From the heart with tears, this is my gift to the special people who have the tremendous honour of paying tribute to a loved one who has passed. When faced with doing a eulogy, time is often limited. Having delivered four eulogies and coached others to create and deliver eulogies, I have created a simple process to help you prepare and deliver a tribute worthy of your loved one.

Visit www.kayleneledgar.com.au/eulogywb to download your FREE copy of:

- From the Heart with Tears workbook for preparing a eulogy.

It's time, take a breath and let's bust your fear.

Self-assessment

IT'S ALL ABOUT YOU

Study everything, but study yourself first.
RALPH SMART

✦ ✦ ✦

Before we dive in to crafting your first speech, let's take a moment to look at where you are as a speaker. The self-assessment provides you with a starting point for you to measure your growth as a speaker.

Learning where you are as a speaker now is the first step to overcome any fear of speaking. The unknown is what gets my heart racing, my mind overthinking and fear consuming me. The more I learnt about speaking and the more I spoke, the more confident I became. This has been true for those that I have mentored and coached over the years as well.

As you progress through the book, you will learn more about each of the 12 skills covered in the self-assessment. You will be challenged to take action to develop your skills and create a speech. It is through taking action that you will gain confidence in each of the skills and overcome the fear of speaking.

For each of the 12 skills you will rate yourself using a scale of 1 to 10, where 1 is the lowest and 10 is the highest. Don't overthink your score, there is no right or wrong answer. Your score is unique to you and used by you to measure your growth. I like to add keywords and comments next to my ratings to help remind me later what was behind the number. I find the rating and the words help me appreciate my improvements when I complete the self-assessment the next time.

The 12 skills covered in the self-assessment are:

- **Busting your fear of public speaking:** How confident are you as a speaker?

- **Getting started:** How confident are you about doing your speech homework?

- **The right package:** How confident are you in defining the purpose and mapping the structure of your speech?

- **Unlocking your story:** How confident are you with storytelling?

- **To Q&A or not:** How confident are you with including a question and answer session in your speech?

- **Bookends matter:** How confident are you with opening your speech to connect and creating a memorable conclusion?

- **Using your voice:** How confident are you with using vocal variety in your speech?

- **Making a move:** How confident are you with making purposeful movements during your speech?

- **Selecting your accessories:** How confident are you with using props, slides and notes in your speech?

- **Let's get social:** How confident are you networking with your audience before and after your speech?

- **Bringing it all together:** How confident are you with practicing your speech?

- **What next?** How confident are you with evaluating your own speech and applying your learnings?

Action: Complete the speaking self-assessment.

Use this template to rate yourself on a scale of 1 to 10 for each skill. A score of 1 means you have no confidence or were unaware of this skill in speaking. A 10 means you are extremely confident and fully implement this skill in all your speeches.

In the thoughts column, note keywords and phrases that come to mind about your current skill level.

Skill	Rating	Thoughts
Busting your fear of public speaking How confident are you as a speaker?		

Skill	Rating	Thoughts
Getting started How confident are you about doing your speech homework?		
The right package How confident are you in defining the purpose and mapping the structure of your speech?		
Unlocking your story How confident are you with storytelling?		
To Q&A or not How confident are you with including a question and answer session in your speech?		
Bookends matter How confident are you with opening your speech to connect and creating a memorable conclusion?		

Skill	Rating	Thoughts
Using your voice How confident are you with using vocal variety in your speech?		
Making a move How confident are you with making purposeful movements during your speech?		
Selecting your accessories How confident are you with using props, slides and notes in your speech?		
Let's get social How confident are you networking with your audience before and after your speech?		
Bringing it all together How confident are you with practicing your speech?		
What next? How confident are you with evaluating your own speech and applying your learnings?		

A final word on self-assessment – it's all about you

This is your journey; you will get out of it what you put in. Go slow or go fast, it is up to you. The key is to follow the process and take up the challenge to face your fear and create your own speech.

CHAPTER 1

Fear Busting

The first step is you have to say that you can.
WILL SMITH

Do you fear public speaking?

Is the fear of public speaking paralysing you?

Are you being held back by your fear of public speaking?

The great news is that public speaking is a learned skill, which means that you can overcome your fear of public speaking. With the right tools and practice you will be able to bust through your fear and speak with confidence.

During this chapter we will explore:

- the fear of public speaking

- why you should bust your fear of public speaking, and

- 5 steps to bust your fear of public speaking.

Glossophobia: The fear of public speaking

When I meet people and talk about my business, I rarely meet someone who is comfortable with public speaking. I would estimate that about 80% of the people I meet fear public speaking to some degree. Most are comfortable living with the fear, while others realise that they need to take steps to break through their fear.

I can relate – for years, I accepted that I had a fear of public speaking. It was normal, it was like my fear of flying and my fear of spiders. I was quite happy to live in my cocoon and not deal with my fears. Then in 2003, I decided that I had to face my fear of public speaking because my need to win a job far outweighed the fear. Similarly, I faced my fear of flying when I wanted to travel overseas. My fear of spiders, however, is NOT something I'm prepared to face.

The fear of public speaking symptoms can vary from person to person, as does the underlying cause of the fear. To help me overcome my fear, I found it useful to reflect on both my symptoms and underlying causes.

Here are 15 'fear of public speaking' symptoms that I have experienced:

- sick feeling in the stomach

- shaking of the knees, hands or body

- sweating

- shortness of breath
- forgetting to breathe when speaking
- talking fast
- accelerated heart rate
- shaky voice
- dry mouth
- overuse of filler words; ums, ahs, so
- nightmares
- unable to sleep
- feelings of panic and anxiousness
- tears, and
- avoiding meetings or events.

When faced with an option 'fight or flight', I would run and not look back. What symptoms have you experienced because of your fear of public speaking?

When I took the time to unpack my fear of public speaking, this is what I found:

- I was concerned that I would look silly, look stupid and make a fool of myself.
- I was concerned that I would say the wrong things, so it was easier to say nothing.
- I was worried about what people would think of me.

- I was worried people would laugh at me.

- I was not sure how to prepare and what to say.

- I was worried I would forget what I was going to say and freeze.

- I doubted my own knowledge and experience; why would anyone want to listen to me?

- I failed at it before, I will fail again.

- I'm not as good as that speaker.

My fear of public speaking began when I was in year 10 English class, then resurfaced when I was 21 and escalated to the point that I struggled to speak in groups of two or more. This was a major problem for me as I wanted to win a job and that meant I had to speak in front of a two-person interview panel.

The underlying cause of our fear is unique to us, our beliefs and our experiences. Taking time to unpack the cause was the first key to me unlocking my fear. Do you know what is behind your fear of public speaking?

Why should you bust your fear of public speaking?

I'm happy never to have to speak in public.

I'm ok not getting that promotion.

It's ok, someone else can give the speech or presentation.

Really, you may want to consider the impact of not taking action to face your fear of public speaking:

- Fear will continue to consume you.

- Your symptoms will continue and likely get more intense.

- Your anxiety and nervousness will surface when you speak.

- Fear will hold you back.

- Others will get opportunities that were meant for you.

- Your unique story will never be shared.

What impact is your fear of public speaking having on you?

On the flip side, by taking action to bust through your fear of public speaking:

- You will learn techniques to help you manage your anxiety and nervousness.

- You will gain confidence as a speaker.

- Your self-confidence will grow and spread to other parts of your life.

- You will be less anxious when presented with a speaking opportunity.

- You will be ready when new opportunities are presented.

- Your unique story will be shared.

What would your life look like without the fear of public speaking? Having overcoming your fear of public speaking, will you be known as an expert in your field? Will more opportunities open up for you at work? Will you be able to honour someone special at a celebration? Will you be able to stand up and give that speech at a loved one's wedding, or funeral? Will you enjoy speaking in front of groups? How important is it to you and your future to bust your fear of public speaking?

I found that the benefits of facing my fear far outweighed the fear itself. Once I started to face my fear, my confidence grew, which helped me in meetings at work as I was able to clearly express my points of view and explain my work in detail. I actually enjoyed attending meetings, especially design sessions where people were encouraged to share their ideas and actively participate in designing new work.

By facing my fear, I was able to not just survive my job interview but exceed expectations by winning a job at a higher pay level. I was still nervous when I attended the interview, however I was able to manage my nerves by taking my time to answer the questions, and I didn't freeze. When new job opportunities came my way, I was ready to take them, without hesitation.

I found myself enjoying speaking in meetings and in front of groups. The more I did it, the more comfortable I became.

I have delivered hundreds of speeches, seminars and workshops. My speeches have been prepared and impromptu and have been from as short as 1 minute to as long as 1 hour. I have spoken in Australia, New Zealand, Malaysia, United States of America and Canada. I have mentored and coached new and experienced speakers for over 10 years. I am a certified World Class Speaking Coach. With all that experience, it may surprise you to hear that I still get nervous, my anxiety does make an appearance and I am comfortable with that. I know how to manage any symptoms that decide to surface. Most importantly, I now embrace that nervous feeling as it means I care. I care about the speech; I care about the audience and I want to give them my best. The day I don't have that nervous feeling before a speech, will be the day I stop speaking.

5 steps to bust your fear of public speaking

Giving a speech may not have been something that you had on your life to-do list. It might be something that you still wish you could avoid. However, at different times in our lives, we do need to speak in front of people. You can overcome your fear of public speaking by following the five steps that helped me.

Step 1: Understand your fear

By understanding your fear of public speaking, you will be in a position to face it and ultimately overcome it.

Take time to reflect and understand why you fear public speaking.

Explore the impact your fear of public speaking is having on your life.

Imagine what life would be like if you did not fear public speaking.

Step 2: Develop your skills to reduce your fear

We fear what we don't know. Therefore, to face your fear, you need to develop your public speaking skills. By reading this book you are already taking steps to develop your skills and reduce your fear of speaking. The tools shared in this book have been broken down into simple steps to help you develop and deliver your speech. As you learn more about speech development and delivery, your confidence will grow and the fear of speaking will reduce.

Darren LaCroix, World Champion of Public Speaking, said during a keynote in Las Vegas 'be a sponge'. What comes to mind when I remember Darren's keynote, is 'absorb all you can, then absorb some more'. This is true when developing your speaking skills.

Read books and articles. Attend workshops and courses. Observe speakers both live and online. Speakers can be anyone, so don't limit your viewing to professional speakers. Speakers are everywhere, at work, in our community, on television and on the radio. When you observe another speaker take note of what you do and don't like about their performance.

You don't want to be a clone of other speakers. Use what you learn to unlock your own unique speaking style. When you start practicing, see what works and doesn't work for you. Go with your gut instinct, what feels right in your tummy, and focus on that.

The journey for developing as a speaker is ongoing. Always embrace the opportunities to learn.

Step 3: Find a support person to help you bust your fear

When I decided to face my fear of public speaking, I signed up for an 8-week Speechcraft Course run by a local Toastmasters Club. The coordinator of the course, Dawn, was key to me overcoming my initial fear of public speaking. Dawn was the person that I turned to when my fear was crushing me and I didn't want to face it anymore. Every time I gave Dawn an excuse why I couldn't do it, she would counter it. Dawn's encouragement, experience and coaching helped me develop my skills as a speaker, build my confidence and break down my fear of speaking. Over the years, I have had many mentors and coaches to help me further develop as a speaker and speaker coach.

Find a support person to help you overcome your fear. Look for someone that will encourage and educate you. You will want to feel comfortable with this person as facing the fear of public speaking is personal and can open up unexpected emotional doors.

While you can do it on your own, having a support person accelerates the process.

Step 4: Visualise speaking without fear

I believe that if you can see it, you can do it. I have found visualisation a powerful tool, not just in overcoming my fear of public speaking, but in other aspects of my life too. I use visualisation to reduce my anxiety of giving a speech. I visualise the full speech, from me walking on to the stage through to when I'm finished and walking off the stage. It is like a dress rehearsal, but in my mind.

Affirmations are another tool that I use. Similar to visualisation, if I say it, I can do it. The mind is wonderful and we can train our brain to believe we can do it. Through the power of positive thoughts, I have been able to reduce my anxiety about speaking and other barriers in my life. The more I repeat an affirmation the more I believe it to be true.

Practice visualisation and affirmations to remove the fear of speaking.

Step 5: Practice, practice, practice until your fear dissolves

To overcome your fear of public speaking, you must speak and speak often.

Find opportunities to speak, start up a conversation with someone you don't know regularly.

If you are like me, you may want to take baby steps. I started by smiling and saying hello to people in the lift at work. As I gained confidence, I would make a comment about the weather or the day of the week.

On Monday, I would say "it is always hard after the weekend".

On Tuesday, I would say "it feels like a Monday".

On Wednesday, I would say "we are halfway through".

On Thursday I had two options, "yay it is pay day", or "one day to go".

On Friday I would say, "I'm looking forward to the weekend, what about you?"

The more people you speak to the easier it will be and your fear will begin to dissolve.

The best decision I made was to join a local Toastmaster Club. As a member of Toastmasters, I gained access to the Toastmasters International program and one step at a time, I developed skills and gained confidence. Toastmasters is a safe place to practice speaking and test new content. As a member you have the opportunity to deliver prepared speeches, impromptu speeches and fulfil meeting roles. As you learn and participate your confidence will grow and your fear will reduce.

You will find opportunities to speak by joining a work, community or sports group committee and being an active member. Speak at committee meetings, connect with members and promote the group at every opportunity.

Volunteer to give the toast or speech at the next family celebration. I did this at my Grandad's 80th birthday celebration at the Melbourne Zoo and this led to other opportunities to speak at family events.

Powerful speeches that connect with the audience will normally have a purposeful story, a story that drives home the major point. Stories take time to develop. Some storylines work with some audiences, and don't work with others. I have found sharing my stories with family and friends provides me with a chance to assess which parts work and which parts need more development. Normally, I just let the story come out naturally in a conversation, however if I'm on a deadline, I will ask if I can test a story.

Action: Understand your fear.

Take time to reflect and understand your fear of public speaking by asking yourself the following questions:

Why do I fear public speaking?

What are my public speaking symptoms?

What would it be like if I didn't fear public speaking?

What am I missing out on because of this fear?

Propel yourself into the future and complete the following statements:

As a confident public speaker, I feel ...

In the past I feared public speaking, now I ...

The best part of overcoming my fear of public speaking is ...

Action: Develop your skills to reduce your fear.

Watch two speakers live or online a week and ask yourself the following:

What do I like about this speaker?

What don't I like about this speaker?

What would I do differently?

How can I adapt _____ to fit with my speaking style?

Action: Find a support person or mentor.

To help you identify a support person or mentor to help you overcome your fear of speaking ask yourself these questions:

Who can I approach to be my support person?

Who do I know that has overcome the fear of public speaking?

Who do I know that is a good speaker?

Action: Practice visualisation and affirmations.

Use these steps to visualise speaking with confidence:

- I am walking on to the stage with confidence, I have a smile on my face and I am wearing ...

- The audience warmly welcomes me as I take a moment and glance around the room.

- I deliver my opening lines and connect with the audience immediately.

- The speech flows naturally and I remember the major points.

- The audience is engaged, they are listening intently and they are smiling back at me.

- There is laughter at the right moments.

- The audience is with me as I re-live my stories. I can see them mirroring my emotions, they really are feeling what I am saying.

- I deliver my final words and the room explodes with a thunderous applause.

- I graciously acknowledge the applause and leave the stage.

- I'm beaming, I did it, I connected with the audience, they got my major points and I feel great.

Practice saying daily affirmations about your speaking success. To help you find the right affirmation for you, try saying the following:

I have a unique story that others need to hear.

I am blessed to have the opportunity to share my story with others.

Today I will share the gift of my experience with . . .

Today I will share my story and the audience will be ready to receive it.

Action: Practice speaking.

Find opportunities to practice speaking regularly by:

Speaking to at least one new person every day.

Find a place where you can practice speaking.

Start telling your stories to family and friends.

A final word on fear busting

Your fear has developed over time, it will not dissolve overnight. Take time to work through each of the five steps to bust through your fear of public speaking. As you do you will become more confident with speaking and the fear will begin to dissolve. Take it one day at a time and you will bust your fear of public speaking. Start speaking today and don't look back.

CHAPTER 2

Getting Started

In spite of your fear, do what you have to do.
CHIN-NING CHU

The first step is often the hardest and the fear of the unknown can prevent you from taking that first step.

During this chapter you will:

- look at why getting started is important
- unlock the pre-event questionnaire, and
- complete the pre-event questionnaire.

Why is getting started important?

Not knowing what is expected when asked to give a speech can have you feeling overwhelmed and feed your fear of speaking.

In my early days as a speaker, I found myself having many a sleepless night, worrying about the unknown. I would stress about what I was going to talk about and who would be in the audience. When I eventually started to prepare my speeches, I would jump in without a clear understanding of my objective and rarely with a known outcome. My preparation for a single speech would take weeks and I would often end up in a completely unexpected place than I originally thought. My speeches were not tight and I often found myself fumbling through them. Back then I did not understand the true value of getting started the right way.

I have since learnt that time well spent at the beginning:

- saves time when preparing a speech

- provides clarity of speech purpose and outcomes

- provides an opportunity to tailor the message for the audience

- eliminates the stress of the unknown and the sleepless nights, and

- lessens the anxiety about the speech and reduces the fear.

I never jump in and book a holiday without researching first. Same goes with a speech, do not jump in and start preparing without doing your research first.

Unlock the pre-event questionnaire

The pre-event questionnaire is a valuable tool for you to gather the necessary information to help you prepare your speech. There are 3 ways to complete the pre-event questionnaire:

- send it to the event organiser and ask them to complete
- you complete the form while speaking to the event organiser, or
- you complete the form.

When approached to give a speech for an organisation, I suggest you either send the form to the organiser to complete or fill it in while you speak to them by phone or in person. When asked to speak at a family event or to deliver a eulogy, I suggest you speak with the family member organising the event to gather information for you to fill in the form. When I organise my own workshops or seminars, I complete the form myself and define my own purpose and outcomes.

The pre-event questionnaire aims to address the following:

- Who asked you to speak?
- When and where will you be speaking?
- Who will you be speaking to?
- What will you be speaking about?
- What additional information do you need?

A sample questionnaire is provided later in this chapter for you to use as is, or to customise to suit your style.

Who asked you to speak?

It is important to have the correct event and group details because if you happen to reference the wrong event or group during your speech it is embarrassing and unprofessional. The more you learn about the event or group, the better prepared you will be when you start creating your speech. Therefore, it is useful to research the event or group before you jump in and start preparing your speech.

It is essential to identify the main contact or event organiser. They will be able to answer any questions that may arise before the event and the day of the event. I encourage you to take time to connect with this person, as this will help you feel more at ease about the presentation. The more comfortable you feel about the presentation the less nervous you will be.

When and where will you be speaking?

The date, time and duration may seem obvious, however imagine if you get this wrong and double book yourself or turn up late or on the wrong day. After preparing your ten-minute speech, you do not want to turn-up to find out that you were scheduled to speak for an hour. Or the reverse, plan an hour speech only to arrive and be told you only have ten minutes. Speakers arriving late, starting late and finishing late are my pet hates. It is disrespectful to the audience, the organiser and other speakers. Always be mindful of time.

When it comes to the venue, you will want the name, address and any specific instructions about parking or finding the venue. If you can visit the venue before the day of the speech, do so, if not check it out using their website or online maps. On the day of your speech, you do not want to be worrying about finding the venue or where to park. If you are worrying, your stress levels are likely to increase and this may impact your nervousness about giving the speech.

Knowing the room layout before the event helps when preparing content and to visualise the delivery of the speech.

The layout of the room can impact on the types of activities used to illustrate a point. Discussion groups and team activities work well with round tables seating however they do not work as well with auditorium style seating. For auditorium style seating, I would avoid team activities and have the audience discuss in pairs or threes but anything bigger would be difficult.

The impact of room layout was highlighted when I was working with a speaker who spent the first 30 seconds of their speech lying on the ground. It was a powerful opening and the audience was hooked immediately. The next time the speech was delivered, the opening was not well received. The difference was room set-up. The first time the room was set-up horseshoe style and everyone in the audience had front row seats. The second time the room was set-up with rows of chairs, those in the front row could see the speaker, those in the second row could see the speaker in part and those in the other rows could not see the speaker.

Speaking from a stage or at audience level can impact on the type of gestures you use during your speech. If you are on a stage it is likely that the audience will see your full body, whereas when speaking from the same level they may only see your upper body.

Knowing if you will be speaking from behind a lectern or having the freedom to move across the stage area will be important when you are focusing on your delivery.

When you are scheduled to speak on the program can influence the content and delivery of the speech. If you are speaking after dinner, you will want to be entertaining and consider adding humour into your speech. If you are speaking after lunch, the audience may be feeling tired and ready for a nap therefore you may want to include more audience engagement.

Who will you be speaking to?

Getting to know who you will be speaking to will help you feel more comfortable.

The size of the audience can influence how you package your content. In a smaller group you may choose to illustrate your point with group activities, whereas in a larger group you may use a story to illustrate the point. The reason for this is that larger groups often require more time for activities as it takes longer to regain control after the activity.

Larger audiences may involve using sound equipment. If so, you will want to discuss this with the event organiser and confirm what equipment they use and if there is an option for testing equipment before the presentation.

The demographic story for each audience will vary and may include information about age, gender, education, professional status and cultures. Let the organiser define the demographic story as they know their audience and what is important to note. If you require specific information about demographics, consider asking more specific questions like:

- average age of attendees
- age range of attendees, and
- cultural mix of attendees.

Two additional questions I like to include are:

- Will most audience members know each other?
- Are they attending by choice or is attendance mandatory?

The answers to these two questions may alter the direction I take when preparing the speech. Where the audience members know each other, I may be able to shine a light on one of the attendees and use their story rather than one of my own. This is where the connection with the event organiser comes in handy. They can help you find the right person to shine the light on and make the connection for you. Shining the light on one of their own is a great way to connect with the audience.

Whether the audience members do or do not know each other, the key is you are aware of this when you are shaping your speech.

It's always nice to know if people are there because they want to be there, or their boss 'voluntold' them to attend. Where people are told to attend, I suggest reaching out to the event organiser to find out why. There is a chance of resistance where a person has been told to attend, and knowing this beforehand means you can be better prepared. The more prepared you are the more confident you will be and the less fear will get in the way.

What will you be speaking about?

When asked to speak, you want to know what is expected from your speech. What is the organiser wanting the audience to do, feel or think after you have spoken? Is there anything specific that they want you to cover or avoid during the speech?

Clarity of purpose and the desired outcomes are the key to creating a high-quality speech. Defining both will help you maintain focus as you develop and deliver your speech.

When you assess the expectations, consider what can realistically be achieved in the allocated time. You may find that the organiser's expectations do not match the time allocated. If that is the case, work with them to identify the priorities, then give them options of what can be delivered. Be clear about what you can and cannot deliver in the specified time - possibly less content in allocated time or more content with increased time allocation. There may be an option to hold a series of sessions.

There may be times when you are given high level, general purposes for the speech and you need to clarify the specific purpose. This is when you need to consider what you can cover in the allocated time; then provide this information to the event organiser and ask them if you have the right purpose.

When you have been asked to speak at a wedding, a family celebration or deliver a eulogy, the purpose may appear clear; toast the happy couple or roast the birthday person or honour the person who has passed.

When I prepare eulogies, I have two purposes. The main purpose is to respectfully honour the person that has passed, an additional purpose is to help those that are grieving. When presenting an award, the main purpose is to honour the recipient and their achievements, an additional purpose may be to inspire others to take action and be considered for future awards.

Whatever the occasion, check with the person who asked you to speak, before you start planning your speech, that you are on the right track.

What additional information do you need?

I used to think that all I needed to know was where I was speaking and what I was speaking about, then I arrived at an event to give my speech titled 'Mastering the Art of Effective Evaluations'. When I was given a copy of the agenda, I saw that the speech was titled 'How to Win an Evaluation Contest'. Awkward, to say the least. Increased stress, absolutely. I had specifically steered away from the win aspect because the focus was the value of an effective evaluation, rather than how to win a contest. To avoid embarrassing myself and the organiser, I had to quickly identify opportunities to link my content to winning contests.

The lesson for me was always be prepared. Know exactly how your speech is being promoted and what the title is on the program. By doing this you will lower the risk of the unexpected and not be faced with extra pressure of last-minute changes.

Action: Complete the pre-event questionnaire.

You can use the sample provided or create your own.

Pre-event questionnaire for [insert your name] presentation

Contact details

Name of event and/or group:	
Contact person name:	
Contact number:	
Contact email:	

Logistics

Date:	
Time and duration:	
Venue name:	
Venue address:	

Venue website, if applicable:	
Are there any specific instructions related to the venue or parking?	
Where will the speech be on the program?	
Room layout:	

Audience

Number of attendees:	
What is the demographic story of attendees?	
Will most attendees know each other?	
Are they attending by choice or is attendance mandatory?	

Presentation objectives

What is the main purpose of the presentation?	
What additional purposes are there?	
What are the desired outcomes from the presentation? What do you want the attendees to think, feel or do?	
Please note any specific topics that you would like included:	
Please note any specific topics that are to be avoided:	

Information to request from organiser

Copy of program.	
Copy of promotional material.	

A final word on getting started

The first step no longer needs to be the hardest. Using the pre-event questionnaire, the fear of the unknown is no longer, as you have the information to create a solid foundation for your speech. Always do your homework, the pre-event questionnaire, before you start planning your speech.

CHAPTER 3

The Right Package

What's loose is lost and what's tight stays in sight.
**CRAIG VALENTINE,
1999 WORLD CHAMPION PUBLIC SPEAKING**

The right package makes all the difference. Your fear of speaking is heightened when you use a loose package, or worse, no package at all.

During this chapter you will:

- see why the right package is essential
- unwrap the right package, and
- map your right package.

Why is the right package essential?

Armed with the information you have gathered in the pre-event questionnaire; it is now time to start mapping out your speech. Using the right package for your speech will keep your content tight and make it easier for you to deliver. You can have the most valuable message in the world, however if it is not packaged right, the message will be lost. After taking the time to share part of yourself with the audience and impart your valuable information, you do not want to risk the key message, your main points, being lost in a messy or loose package.

With the right package, it will be easier for you to remember your main points, and therefore reduce your fear of speaking. You do not need to worry about, "What am I going to say?" or "What comes next?"

The risk of not having the right package is that you will feel less confident when you are delivering your presentation. During your presentation you may forget what is next because your content is loose and does not flow. You may lose your way and go off on a tangent, or worse, draw a blank. The risk of any of these happening is enough to increase your fear of speaking.

Unwrapping the right package

The overall structure of the speech will include an opening, body with three main points and a conclusion. The opening sets the scene and lets the audience know what is to come. The conclusion is what the audience hears last and drives home your overall message. The body is your three main points, your gifts to the audience. The body is developed first, and when you have a clear picture of your body, you can then work on your opening and conclusion.

As you unwrap the right package you will:

- define your overall message
- identify your main points, and
- apply the PAR formula to your main points.

Using the completed pre-event questionnaire, it is now time to start working on the speech structure beginning with the end in mind, the overall message.

Defining your overall message

The overall message is what the audience will leave with after having heard your speech. Will they think differently? Will they feel differently? Will they do something different? It is a single statement that will capture the essence of the speech in 10 words or less.

Defining the overall message will keep you focused as you prepare and deliver your speech. If a story, an activity, or any content does not support the overall message, then it does not belong in the speech. Remembering this will help you deliver a tight speech with a clear purpose; the audience won't be left wondering 'what was that about'. Your message will be received and remembered.

Owning your overall message will give you confidence, and this confidence will build as you create your speech. Step-by-step your fear will begin to evaporate because you have taken the time to get this right.

To create the overall message, use the pre-event questionnaire main purpose, additional purpose and desired outcome. When you are able to capture the essence of the speech in 10 words or less, your overall purpose will be crystal clear.

Your overall message will be your working speech title. After you have drafted and refined your speech, you will know if this will be your actual title or you may uncover another title.

Identifying your main points

The next step to create a solid foundation for your speech is to uncover the main points. The main points will form the body of the speech and must support your overall message. Three main points work well – you do not want to overwhelm the audience with information overload.

To identify the main points, brainstorm topics and points that would support the overall message. You may have three points that jump out at you straight away. Other times you may need to look for similarities and group them to narrow down the list of topics and points to choose from. Like the overall message for the speech, you want each main point to be crystal clear.

Once you have your 3 main points, you need to consider the order they will be presented. You want the information to flow, to be easy for you to deliver and the audience to follow. In World Class Speaking we call this the Roadmap. You may find there is a natural order like step 1, step 2 and step 3. Sometimes there is no clear order, and this is when you can get creative. You can use 3 steps or you could use 3 keys, 3 tools, 3 doors or 3 stepping stones. As you work on your main points you may uncover an acronym, like PAR – Point, Anchor and Reflection. Your speech theme may provide a natural link to the roadmap. If your speech was about travel you could use destination, 3 stops or 3 ports. Alternatively, you could use, the first stop on our trip will be… then we will visit… and finally we will arrive at…

The key is to provide a roadmap for your speech that the audience will easily follow from start to finish.

Applying the PAR formula

The next step for the solid foundation is to apply the World Class Speaking PAR formula to each of the 3 main points. PAR stands for point, anchor and reflection. The 3 elements of the PAR formula when packaged together produce a solid point that will be easy for you to deliver and the audience to remember.

The process is to firstly apply the PAR formula to each of your main points, one at a time. Then you can start to write your speech beginning with each of your main points.

The length of your speech will determine how much content you can include for each main point. For a 45-minute speech you may allow 4 to 6 minutes for the opening and close, with approximately 13 minutes per main point. For a 10-minute speech, you might allow 1 to 2 minutes for the opening and close, with approximately 2 to 3 minutes per main point.

Point

Before you can start shaping your content, you need to fully understand the main point. The more clarity you have about the main point, the more confident you will be to create and deliver the material. The more confident you are the less you will fear speaking.

Once you are clear on the point, you want to capture the essence of the point in a single phrase or headline. This is the take-away message for this main point. The phrase or headline needs to be easy for you to remember and repeatable. You want the audience to remember it long after your presentation. Think of this like a headline for a newspaper article. Headlines are often catchy, intriguing and capture the point of the story in a few words. You see the headline and you want to read the article. With your speech you want the audience to hear the headline and remember the main point.

Aim to keep phrases to ten words or less. Make the phrase easy to comprehend – if a child can understand your phrase then an audience should grasp it easily. I have been known to test my phrases on my nine-year-old niece – she likes to be involved and it helps me tighten my phrases. I enlisted her help to test the chapter titles for this book. Based on her feedback I changed chapter 4 from the original title of 'authentic connection' to 'unlock your story'. I knew the new chapter title was right when she said "it's like your stories are treasurers and when you open the box, they all come out". If you can enlist the support of a child, do so, as children truly bring magic into the world. Test your phrase with family members or friends too, and see if they get the point without you having to explain it.

Rhythmic phrases roll off your tongue easier and are pleasant to the ear. "Winners are grinners" sounds better than "People who win feel good". Short sharp phrases are easy to recall and can pack a punch. "No regrets" sounds better than "The turning point in my life".

I find it useful to spend time brainstorming phrases before deciding on the phrase. Do not worry if the phrase is not coming to you immediately, it will reveal itself as you develop your point. If the phrase is not quite right, that is fine, it can be tweaked as you develop the point further.

The key is to ensure that you clearly understand the main point, what you want the audience to walk away with. Use the main point and the phrase as your compass to keep your content on the right track. As you develop your content, ask yourself 'does this support the main point, the phrase, the headline?' If it does not, then leave it out.

Anchor

You want all of your content to be purposeful, to add value and support your main point, otherwise your message can get lost. Using an anchor will help your audience understand and remember your point.

The 3 anchors that I use to drive home my points are:

- anecdote
- activity, and
- acronym.

My go to is the anecdote, the story. People connect through stories. I read books, listen to audio books and watch movies to escape into stories. Listening to my grandma re-live stories of her childhood when she spent hours in bomb shelters during World War II. Listening to my dad re-live his adventures as a child climbing up a cliff. Listening to my six-year-old nephew tell me stories about him and Darth Vader saving the day. The magic is in being transported to a different place and time. Grandma and Dad re-lived their stories, while my nephew used his imagination. Both techniques were effective because they were delivered with passion. When using a story to make your point, you want to re-live the story, invite the audience into the story and let them be part of it. A well-crafted story will be remembered and therefore your point will be remembered too.

When I can, I enjoy using an activity to make the point. Inviting the audience to participate in an activity and for them to realise the point themselves is a great way to make your point stick. The key to a successful activity is how you frame it, how you set it up. The instructions you provide to the audience must be clear. The challenge is selecting the right activity to make your point. When selecting an activity, you will need to consider the size of the audience and time available. As mentioned in chapter 2 the room layout can influence the type of activity used to illustrate your point. Discussion groups and team activities work well with round table seating or where there is space for the attendees to stand up and form groups. Whether you do table activities or activities in pairs, the more people in attendance, the more time you will need to regain control after the activity.

A quick and effective activity to highlight that change feels uncomfortable is to ask the audience to 'fold their arms', then after a few moments ask them to 'fold their arms the other way'.

In my bust your fear of speaking workshops, I use an interview and introduction activity to help the attendees start to break through their fear of public speaking. In pairs, I ask the attendees to interview each other, then they are to introduce their partner to the group. After the interview part of the activity, I highlight to them that they have taken the first step to breaking through their fear by talking to their partner, someone they just met. I then invite them one by one to introduce their partners. At the end of the introductions, I congratulate them all for their first mini speech in front of the group. I use the activity to reinforce the point that they can speak in public and survive.

Occasionally, I will use an acronym to make my point. An acronym is using the first letter of each sub-point to form another word. When my speech includes a main point on goal setting, I use the acronym SMARTER; Specific, Measurable, Action Orientated, Realistic, Time-bound, Evaluate progress and Reward. Using the acronym helps the audience members to recall the steps for setting their goals.

When identifying which anchor you will use, specify the anchor with a brief description. Here are examples I have used:

- Anecdote – What triggered my change?

- Activity – Folding arms, change is uncomfortable.

- Acronym – SMARTER goals.

Reflection

Reflection is when the audience connects their life, their situation with your point. As a speaker you can prompt the reflection with a well-placed thought-provoking question. When speaking about my fear of public speaking and the impact it had on my life, my reflection question is 'what are you missing out on because of your fear?' followed by 'imagine your fear was no longer, what could you achieve?' When I ask these questions, I am not expecting the audience to give me the answer, I am wanting them to take a moment to look within and answer the question for themselves.

One reflection question is sufficient; however, I like to use two. The first question gets the audience reflecting on the pain, the result if they do not take action or learn the lesson. The second question gets them to reflect on the relief, the result of taking action or learning the lesson. This reflection process helps the audience member buy-in to the point and want to experience the relief, the benefit for themselves.

A good reflection question will bring the audience into your speech – they will connect with the point and see how it relates to them. Connecting with the audience, opening the door for them to have their own a-ha moments, will boost your confidence and catapult you away from your fear.

Your anchor may be a reflection activity. This can be an effective way to drive home your point while letting the audience members take the driver's seat.

Identifying your transition statements

A smooth transition statement will help your speech flow, reinforce the last point and get the audience ready for the next part of your speech. As you create your main points, think about how you will reinforce the point and move smoothly to the next. After the final point the transition statement will lead to the conclusion.

Let's look at transitions for a speech with the following 3 main points:

1. Facing your fear of public speaking.

2. Developing your speech.

3. Delivering your speech.

Moving from main point 1 to main point 2:

"Having locked the door on your fear, are you ready to open the door and see how to create your speech?"

Moving from main point 2 to main point 3:

"Armed with your speech tools, it's now time to lift the curtain and walk on to the stage."

Moving from main point 3 to conclusion:

"Delivering a speech is more than words, it is a performance, take a bow and exit stage right."

Ideally the transition statement will be one sentence, however it can be two. The key is to make it smooth and flow naturally to the next part of the speech.

Action: Define your overall message.

To define your overall message ask yourself:

- What do I want my audience to leave with at the end of the speech?

- In ten words or less, how can I capture the essence of my speech?

Using the mapping your right package template, fill-in your overall message.

Action: Identify your roadmap.

To identify your main points ask yourself:

- What are 3 main points for my speech?

- Using these 3 main points, what roadmap can I provide the audience to help them follow the speech?

Using the mapping your right package template, fill-in your 3 main points in the order you will present them.

Action: Use the PAR formula for your main points.

Complete the following for each of your 3 main points.

Defining your point

To gain clarity about each of your 3 main points finish these statements:

- This point is important because ...

- The audience needs to hear this point because ...

- After hearing this point the audience will ...

To define your phrase or headline ask yourself:

- In ten words or less, what is the exact point I want the audience to walk away with?

Using the mapping your right package template, fill-in your phrase or headline for each main point.

Identifying your anchor

To identify which type of anchor to use ask yourself:

- How did I learn the point?
- How will I illustrate my point?
- What anecdote, activity or acronym will I use?

Using the mapping your right package template, fill-in the anchor you will use for each main point along with a brief description.

Identifying your reflection piece

To identify a reflection piece ask yourself:

- What question can I ask to get my audience to think about their own situation in respect of this point?

Using the mapping your right package template, fill-in your reflection piece for each main point.

Action: Identify your transition statements.

To identify your transition statements for each main point ask yourself:

- How can I reinforce this point while getting the audience ready for the next?

Using the mapping your right package template, fill-in your transition statements.

Action: Complete the map your right package template.

Overall message is: _____

First main point is: _____

    Phrase/Headline: _____

    Anchor: _____

    Reflection piece: _____

    Transition statement: _____

Second main point is: _____

    Phrase/Headline: _____

    Anchor: _____

    Reflection piece: _____

    Transition statement: _____

Third main point is: _____

    Phrase/Headline: _____

    Anchor: _____

    Reflection piece: _____

    Transition statement: _____

Action: Write your speech.

Using the right package map, start to write your speech beginning with the main points. Connect your main points using your transition statements.

If you prefer, use voice to text software, and speak out your main points, then review and clean-up the transcript.

If you are using an anecdote as your anchor, I suggest you read the next chapter, 'unlock your story', first.

A final word on the right package

Keep your content tight and relevant by ensuring all main points support the overall message. Use a phrase or headline to keep your main points focused. Anchor your message with an anecdote, activity or acronym to help your audience remember your content. Encourage your audience to reflect and personally connect to you point.

Using the right package will give you confidence and make it easier for you to recall your content.

CHAPTER 4

Unlock Your Story

> There is no greater agony than
> bearing an untold story inside you.
> **MAYA ANGELOU**

✦ ✦ ✦

We all have stories inside us. We just have to take time to unlock them. Stories are one of the most powerful tools to anchor your main points. We love to listen to stories. We love to immerse ourselves in a good book, in a good movie. Stories told in speeches have that same effect. With a well-told story your audience will go into that story and they will re-live the story with you. That will create a greater connection to you and your main point. Having the audience with you will ease any nervousness and help to lift any remaining fear.

During this chapter you will:

- look at why you should use stories
- be introduced to the power of 6Cs, and
- unlock your own story.

Why use stories to make your point?

Stories are the most popular anchor for driving home a point. The audience will remember your story; therefore, they will remember your main point. Tell a story, make a point. Tell a story, make a point. It is an effective tool to be able to ensure that your message is received and goes home with the audience member.

The benefit of having a story within your speech is that you know your own stories, you do not have to think, "What am I going to say next?" You lived the story therefore you are able to re-live the story. You have told the story to your family, your friends and now you can share it with an audience. The story comes from within therefore you are less nervous about that part of your speech.

I have seen many a nervous speaker begin their speech with visible nerves, then as they start to re-live their story, the nerves lift and they are like a new speaker. I believe re-living your stories is one of the most effective ways to overcome your fear of speaking. When you are in the moment of your story, it is hard to think about how nervous you were feeling. Fear of speaking diminishes when you re-live your story as you do not stress or overthink about what to say next.

When sharing your story, you are in a position where you are able to naturally connect with your audience. You do not need to memorise your speech word for word, because it is your story and you have internalised it. You know your story; you have shared it before and you have practiced the delivery. There is no right or wrong with your story, because you are re-living what you experienced.

Power of 6Cs

Why are some stories more powerful than others? The answer is that powerful stories contain 6 key elements:

- characters
- circumstance
- conflict
- cure
- change, and
- carry-out message.

When a story contains these 6 elements, you have a story that will connect with the audience and drive home your main point. To test your story, answer the following 6 questions with a single statement:

- Who are the characters in the story?
- What is the circumstance behind your story?
- What was the conflict?
- What was the cure?
- What happened to change things going forward?
- What is the carry-out message?

When you can answer these 6 questions with clarity, you have a story that you can nurture and create into a powerful story that will connect with your audience.

When unlocking your story, think back to when you first learnt the lesson or realised the point. How did you learn it? Did you read it somewhere? Did someone give you the advice? What is your first memory of learning this point? The magic comes from recalling and then re-living the first moment you realised the point. Remember what it was like before you learnt the lesson. Recall what changed after the lesson was learnt – how did you change, what changed for you.

To create your powerful story, clearly define the 6Cs of your story.

Characters

Who are the characters in your story?

As it is your story, one of the characters is likely to be you. Who else is in your story?

Why are characters important in your story? The audience will relate to and connect with the characters. Give your characters a name, describe what they look like and their personality to help the audience see them come alive.

Leave some information out to allow the audience to fill in the blanks. This allows the audience to immerse themselves within your story.

When coaching clients, I demonstrate this point by using a surfer on a beach. I ask my client to tell me about the surfer:

- What colour hair did the surfer have?
- What were they wearing?
- What colour was the clothing?
- If they mention a surfboard, what colour was it?
- Was the surfer male or female?

The number of questions I ask depends on the time available.

The client shares their surfer with me, then I tell them my image of the surfer which is never the same as their surfer. Most of the time the surfer is male, in shorts with a tank top on but that is where the similarities finish. Over the year the surfer has had blonde hair, brown hair, short hair, long hair, dreadlocks, dry hair and wet hair. They have been dressed in blue shorts, board shorts, denim cut-off shorts, red tank top, blue muscle top, no top or in a wetsuit. Some surfers had surfboards and others did not. The point of the exercise is that by allowing them to connect with the surfer and fill in their own description they connected with the character. The conversation that follows explores how they felt when I told them that my surfer was different. Most express some level of disappointment and disconnect with my surfer. They all agree that by allowing them to co-create the surfer, they felt more engaged and part of the story.

When introducing your character, share important characteristic, plant the seeds of the character and then allow the audience to complete the picture themselves.

There may be occasions where you are unable to use the characters real name. In these cases, give them a new name – you can be creative. When I speak about children, I will often refer to them as Miss M or Master six-year-old, rather than using their name.

Including characters in your stories provides the opportunity to add dialogue, introduce vocal variety and spark interest with your audience. You can naturally unlock humour through your characters dialogue.

I like to use inner dialogue, where I am having a conversation with myself or sharing with the audience what is going through my mind at a particular moment in the story.

Circumstance

What is the circumstance behind your story?

This is where you paint the picture and set the scene for the story. When painting the picture, think about what you can hear, see, feel and smell in the scene. As mentioned earlier, leave some information out to allow the audience to complete the picture themselves.

Find an opportunity to invite the audience into the situation. Will they be walking towards you in the street or looking out their window as you walked past? Were they standing there when you got in the car or will they be in the car with you? There is a subtle difference between having the audience watching the scene to having them in the scene.

The audience is watching the scene when I say:

> I was in the car driving ...

The audience is in the scene when I say:

> If you were sitting next to me in the car as I drove ...

The scene is the same but how I set it up is different.

Conflict

What was the conflict?

Conflict can take on many forms, it may be between you and the other character, you and a third person or the conflict may be an internal battle.

Conflict will draw the audience in therefore you will want to establish this early in your story. As the conflict escalates the audience will be hanging on to your every word. The path to the climax of your story, the cure, needs to be hard. You want the audience to feel your pain, your discomfort, your need to break through the conflict. The more you intensify the conflict, the more the audience will be on your side, wanting you to find a solution, willing you to overcome the challenge.

The clearer you are about the conflict, the deeper the connection with the audience. Reflect on what you felt, saw and heard at the time. What led to the conflict? What impact was it having on your life? The deeper you go into the conflict, the more powerful it will be when you re-live it with your audience.

Cure

What was the cure?

The cure is the solution, the catalyst for change. You have lifted the audience to the climax, now you give them the relief by sharing who cured the conflict, what solved the problem. Did the other character say something to you, teach you something? What was the turning point? The a-ha moment when the lesson was learnt. This may be the phrase or headline you created while working through the PAR formula. As you work on clarifying the cure, you may find a stronger phrase or headline for this main point.

During a conversation with the other character, did they give you the cure or say something that had you recalling a seed that was planted in the past by someone else?

When looking into the cure, you may need to dig deep and go back in time to identify when the seed for the cure was planted. Sometimes the seed may have been planted years earlier by a family member, friend, work colleague, something you saw on television or read in a book.

Bring the emotion out – how did you feel at the time, how did you feel immediately afterwards? Why was this the turning point?

Change

What happened to change things going forward?

It is not just enough to let your audience know that you overcome the conflict. Relieve their curiosity by sharing with them how things changed for you afterwards. You want the audience to feel the relief, to be excited about the change and to want it for themselves. As they hear how you benefited from the change, you want them to be thinking, 'wow it could happen to me too'.

Carry-out message

What is the carry-out message?

After the audience has listened to your story, what is the message that they will take-away? This message may be the words provided in the cure or it could be the phrase or the headline you created when using the PAR formula. The message should be easy for the audience to grasp and remember.

The 6Cs at work

Let's look at my fear of public speaking story and see if I have incorporated the 6Cs.

> It was a cold, wet Monday night in the middle of winter. I was scheduled to speak at the second night of an eight-week public speaking course. I had survived the first week, barely. I could still feel the terror of that first night when I had to say my name. I stood-up, blurted out my name and collapsed into the chair. I had spoken but there was no relief, I still felt sick to the stomach and the shaking continued until it was time to leave.

Tonight, I was to give my first speech, my ice-breaker speech. The speech was to be about me – easy, right? If you were with me, in my warm cosy car, as I approached the venue, you would have sensed the fear in the air as I drove straight past the entrance. I drove around the block and as I came near the entrance a second time, you would have heard me say out loud "I'm going in. I'm going in." as I kept driving past. On the third trip around the block you would have witnessed me having a conversation with myself. "I'm going in this time. I have to do it." Then my reply, "No, you don't!" as I kept driving. It was like the driveway entrance wasn't there.

After the fourth time I decided I could not go to the course and I rang the course coordinator, a beautiful woman named Dawn. I said to Dawn, "I'm sorry, Dawn, I just can't do this. I can't come tonight." Dawn asked, "Why not, Kaylene?" and I responded, "I feel sick." Dawn asked, "Why do you feel sick, Kaylene?" To which I sighed and then blurted out, "Because I can't give my speech. I can't talk in front of that group of people. I'm just … I feel sick. I'm too nervous. I can't do it." Dawn wasn't going to let me off that easy and said "Okay, Kaylene, tell me what you were going to say. Tell me about you." Taking a deep breath, I began, "Well, I planned to tell them about my family. I was going to talk about my Mum, and my Dad, and that I have two younger brothers. I was going to talk about why I'm here living in Canberra while my family is in Melbourne. I thought I could then talk a bit about my job and what I like about it and why I'm here at this course. Then, I thought I'd tell them about what I'm interested in, because I really like nature and animals. That's it, that is what I was going to say, but I just … I can't do it in front of them. I can't stand up and speak."

Dawn in her steadying, calming grandmother tone replied, "Kaylene dear, you just gave your speech. You just did it. You can do this. You can do this tonight." I didn't believe her and said "No, I can't." Dawn was determined to get me there and said in her don't test me tone, "Yes, you can." I hesitated then said, "Really? You think I can do this?" Dawn, back to her loving grandmother tone, said "Yes, you can. You can do this, Kaylene. It's time to share your story."

Wow, it's time to share my story! My story! Dawn believed in me and she had only just met me the week before. Dawn was a beautiful, articulate speaker and she believed in me, she told me I can do it. She said it's time to share my story.

On the fifth turn I entered the driveway. I went in. I was terrified. I felt sick in the stomach. I thought I was going to vomit or faint, the shakes were uncontrollable but I did deliver my first speech. Dawn was right, I could do it. I just needed Dawn to make me believe that I could. I needed that extra person to give me some confidence, because I had none. When Dawn gave me that bit of confidence, that bit of reassurance that I could do it, I started to believe that I could speak.

Over the remaining weeks of the course my nerves slowly began to reduce. The fear of speaking was still there but it was not as intense as it was before the course. I started to learn how to craft a speech, how to find the right words and how to manage my nerves. To my surprise at the end of the course I did feel more confident and was sad to see the end. The reason I had joined the course in the first place was to give me confidence to speak at upcoming job interviews, I wanted to secure a level 5 position and stay in Canberra. While I was nervous entering the interviews, I was able to manage my nerves and answer all questions with confidence. I won not one but three jobs – the first two were level 5 promotions and the third was, to my amazement, a level 6 promotion. By facing my fear, I was able to exceed my expectations with the job interviews and secure a higher than expected position. This made me think, 'what could I do if I continued to face the fear', then I heard Dawn's voice "You can do this! It is time to share your story." I rang Dawn and organised to visit her Toastmasters Club that week. I joined on my first night and never looked back.

With the right support, with the right tools, you can conquer your fears and realise your potential. You just have to remember what Dawn said "You can do it! It's time to share your story."

Does my story have the 6Cs? Let's do the test.

- Who are the characters in the story? Dawn the course coordinator and me.

- What is the circumstance behind your story? I am in my car heading to speak at the second night of an eight-week public speaking course and my fear starts to consume me.

- What was the conflict? My fear of public speaking preventing me entering the driveway.

- What was the cure? Dawn telling me "You can do it! It's time to share your story."

- What happened to change things going forward? I was able to give my first speech, start to overcome my fear and I won three jobs.

- What is the carry-out message? With the right support, you can do it because it's time to share your story.

As you can see, I can clearly express the essence of this story by answering the 6 questions. This is how I know the story will connect. I have shared this story over the years, and I know it sticks because ten years after I first told this story, I heard a person from the audience that day re-telling my story to make their point.

Did you notice the dialogue between the characters? Did you hear my inner dialogue?

Did you see the conflict building as my fear started to consume me, as I kept driving around the block? Did you notice that I invited you into the car with me? You were not just sitting on the sideline watching this unfold, you were with me in the car.

Who said the most important words in the story, "You can do it! It's time to share your story"? Not me, Dawn. She was the hero not me. I needed Dawn to make the break through.

The carry-out message is clearly "You can do it! It's time to share your story". With the right support and tools, you can achieve whatever you set your mind to. You have made the decision to pick up this book and start to overcome your fear of speaking. Remember, as Dawn says, "You can do it! It's time to share your story."

Unlocking your story

I used to think my stories were boring. Then Rebecca, a friend and fellow Toastmaster, opened my eyes when she told me "you just think your stories are boring because you have heard them so many times before." This changed how I saw my stories. I started to enjoy sharing stories. I began to appreciate that when you share your story with a new audience, they are living it for the first time. It is a new adventure for them and therefore it is not boring.

Craig Valentine, co-founder of the World Class Speaking Coach certification program, introduced me to the 'Story File'. A story file is where you record the highlights, the essence of your stories. When you see something that means something to you, that connects with your heart, that has a profound impact on you, note it in your Story File. Keep your eyes and ears open, for there are stories all around you.

You do not need to write out the full story, you just need to capture sufficient information for you to recall it later when you are ready to unlock the story. I have found noting the following helps me:

- Who are the characters? Brief description of them.

- What is the circumstance behind your story? What did I see, hear, smell, touch or do?

- What was the conflict? What happened? How did it make me feel?

- What was the cure? How did I feel when the cure was realised?

- What change happened as a result of the cure?

- What would be the carry-out message?

I have a smart phone where I have created a Story File folder in the notes app. I create a new note for each story. Alternatively, you might like the traditional way of having a notebook in your pocket so that you can jot things down. The method is not important, the action is. Find the method that works for you and start capturing your stories today.

In addition to the Story File, you can create other types of files. I have created a Humour File to capture humorous stories, sayings and jokes. I also have a Quote File where I capture quotes by famous people as well as quotes from people I meet.

Action: Unlock your story.

Step 1: Answer the following 6 questions with a single statement.

- Who are the characters in the story?
- What is the circumstance behind your story?
- What was the conflict?
- What was the cure?
- What happened to change things going forward?
- What is the carry-out message?

Step 2: Write your story.

Write the story how you would say it. You may prefer to use voice to text software which is my preference. I find it easier to tell my story as it flows naturally when I say it. When I type my stories, I find myself overthinking each sentence and it makes the process longer.

Step 3: Review and polish your story.

When I say this, I do not mean changing the essences of the story or the facts. Your story must remain authentic. What you want to do is polish the words, add descriptive language, to help paint the pictures. Look at how the story unfolds – have you clearly expressed the pain to the cure? Have you used dialogue, are you re-living the story or are you just telling the story?

Step 4: Share your story.

Practice your story by sharing it with family and friends. Get their reaction, see what works and what does not. When you are re-living the story, can you see them feeling your pain, are they curious as to what will happen? Do you notice the relief when you share the cure? Are they connecting with the change? Can they repeat the carry-out message easily?

You may want to record yourself sharing the story and then review the recording. I find this particularly useful as it highlights where I need to add pauses, emphasis or where I need to add more descriptions to paint the picture more clearly. Tighten your story and make any additional updates.

The more you share your story the more comfortable you will be sharing it with others. The story is a part of you, the more you share it the more your confidence will grow.

Step 5: Package your story in your speech.

Now you have your story, where will it be included in your speech? I personally like the method of telling a story then making your point. That said, sometimes it works better to make the point, then use the story to reinforce the point. As you pull your speech together you will work out where it fits best.

A final word on unlock your story

Stories are all around us, every day. Open your eyes to the magic and capture your stories in your Story File. Use the 6Cs to re-live your story and your audience will join you. Sharing my stories helped me gain confidence and overcome my fear of speaking. This can be true for you. Remember Dawn's words, "You can do it! It's time to share your story."

In the words of my nine-year-old niece, "your stories are treasures and when you open the box, they all come out."

CHAPTER 5

To Q & A or Not

Sometimes questions are more important than answers.
NANCY WILLARD

❖ ❖ ❖

It's hard enough doing a speech and now I need to think about allowing the audience to ask me questions.

Overcoming my fear of speaking and learning how to prepare and deliver my speeches had given me confidence. Then I was thrown a curveball - "Kaylene after your speech, there will be time for a 10-minute Q & A". What? All my fear of speaking came back to me in an instant. I had seen many question and answer session before and as a member of the audience I rarely participated. Now I was going to lead the session and I felt sick.

The thought of having to do a Q & A session filled me with dread. My main concern was not being able to answer their questions, followed by stumbling over my answer. I was sickly concerned about audience members being negative and heckling me during the session. I didn't want to look stupid. I didn't want to lose control.

To my surprise, I survived that first Q & A and have now learnt to enjoy the opportunity. If doing a Q & A session is something that gets your heart racing, fills you with fear, the good news is with the right preparation and tips you can comfortably lead a successful Q & A session.

During this chapter you will:

- consider if a Q & A session is required

- learn the importance of Q & A session placement, and

- gain tips on preparing and managing a successful Q & A session.

Is a Q & A session needed?

Not all presentations require a Q & A.

I am not going to include a Q & A session when invited to speak at a wedding, a funeral or a birthday celebration. I will include a Q & A session when invited to speak about 'busting your fear of public speaking' or 'unlocking your story'.

When invited to speak at an event, the organiser may ask you to include a Q & A or they may invite you to be part of a speaker Q & A panel.

When you are invited to participate on a speaker Q & A panel, you do not need to include a Q & A in your presentation. A speaker Q & A panel will have a moderator who facilitates the session. The moderator will often allow each of the speakers a final word before wrapping up.

Where you have not been asked to include a Q & A, you can decide if one is required or not.

When deciding if you will include a Q & A or not ask yourself the following:

- Will having a Q & A add value to your presentation and audience engagement?

- Will the audience want to ask questions and share their thoughts?

- If you don't have a Q & A, how can audience members connect with you if they have questions or want more information?

A Q & A session can add value to your presentation as it provides an opportunity for the audience members to interact with you and open a conversation about the topic. Allowing the audience to ask any burning questions about the topic, to seek clarification on a point or to ask a question about a related topic, brings them into the presentation and gives them a chance to be heard. As a speaker you gain valuable insight as to how your main points are being received. The questions asked may highlight new content for inclusion in future presentations. The types of questions asked will provide an insight into how your message has been received.

If time does not allow for a Q & A or you decide not to include one, you may consider one of these options for attendees to ask their questions:

- Make yourself available after the presentation to answer questions one to one.

- Invite the attendees to email you any questions.

- Invite them to follow you on Social Media and to private message you any questions.

You may also consider using one of these at the end of your Q & A session, if there were more questions than time allowed.

If you decided to use an alternate method for managing questions, it may be useful to let the audience know up front either during your opening or have the person introducing you provide the instructions on your behalf.

Whether you do or do not include a Q & A session in your presentation, you will find value in the tips on how to prepare for questions.

Where to place the Q & A session?

The Q & A always goes after the speech, right?

I suggest you do not place the Q & A session after your speech. While the Q & A is often placed there, there is a risk that you will lose control over what your audience hears last. After having prepared a powerful presentation that makes your audience think and ready to take action, you want them to leave hearing your words last. If you place the Q & A after your conclusion, you lose that opportunity and risk them leaving on a different point or worse still, a negative one.

For this reason, it is important to place the Q & A session not at the very end of your presentation. Placing it before your conclusion will allow you the opportunity to conclude the Q & A and re-focus the audience on you and your topic before delivering your conclusion, your final message.

Tips on preparing and managing a successful Q & A session

The fear of losing control during a Q & A session will escalate as the date of your presentation nears if you don't take time to prepare. Use these tips to prepare and manage the Q & A session and you will set yourself up for a successful session.

Potential questions and answers

Using the information you gathered in the pre-event questionnaire and your knowledge of the topic, brainstorm possible questions the audience may ask. Consider engaging the event organiser to find a few attendees that you can work with before the event to gather information that will help your presentation development as well as identify possible questions. Utilise your network, your family and friends, ask them what questions they might have related or unrelated to the topic. The related and unrelated topics are important as this will help you prepare for the curveball questions, the unexpected question that is not on your radar.

Review the list of potential questions, and be on the lookout for important information that supports your main points. If not already included in your presentation, consider whether adding it will add value to your presentation and drive home the main point.

The remaining questions, while valid, may not add additional value – they may not even support the main points of the speech. Prepare answers for these questions. Keep your answers short and to the point. Practice answering the questions. One technique I have used in the past is to have each question printed on a business card size piece of paper. Randomly I would select a question and practice my answer.

Silence, no questions

Oh no, I finally got the courage to include a Q & A session in my presentation and there is silence, no one has a question. Don't skip to the conclusion! Share one of the prepared questions and answers, and make sure it is one that will add value, not a curveball question. Doing this may open the door for the audience to start asking questions.

You can set-up your question as follows:

- "I'm often asked…"
- "Recently I was asked…"

After you have provided the question and answer, you can put to the audience "what are your thoughts on that?" and hold eye contact with an audience member that may have been nodding or smiling in agreement. The eye contact may prompt them to agree or disagree and then add their thoughts.

Another technique is to turn the Q & A into a debrief, where you use the questions to engage the audience into sharing their experiences. To do this the follow-up question may be "what would you do in that situation?"

If silence is something that you fear or are just concerned about, you may want to look at prompting a few attendees to be prepared to ask questions. If you worked with a few attendees when preparing the presentation, they may have raised a question or topic that you are not going to cover or only partially cover. You could suggest to them that they may want to raise the question during the Q & A. Even better, you could treat it like a press conference and offer to give them the first question, make them feel important.

You will often find that once you get the first question out there, the doors open, and more questions will come in.

Oh no, I don't know the answer

You are human! Just because you have been invited to speak on the topic and you are seen as an expert does not mean you know everything about the particular topic.

It is reasonable to expect that you may be faced with a question that you do not know the answer to, a question that did not make it on your potential question list, a question you have never been asked.

When faced with this situation, it is a perfect opportunity to throw the question to the audience. Invite them to help answer the question, let one of the attendees shine and be the hero. To do this you can acknowledge the question and that you do not have an answer or have not had that experience, then put the question to the audience. Consider phrasing your response as follows:

- "Great question, I have not come across that before, (turn to the rest of the audience) do you have any thoughts on that question?"

- "Good question, (turn to the audience), what do you think? Have you experienced that situation? I'd love to hear how you handled it too."

Having the confidence to admit you do not have all the answers, and allow another to be the hero and give the answer, is classy and helps build rapport with the audience.

If you or the audience cannot provide an answer to the question, consider a response like:

- "Great question. I have not thought about that before. Let me have some time to think about it and I will get back to you after this session."

If you do this ensure you get their contact details after the session, so that you can follow-up with them. An alternative is to say that you will look into it and provide a response to the event organiser to share with everyone.

The key is to be honest – never make up an answer. If you don't know, then you don't know. Add this to your potential questions for next time.

Dealing with challenging situations

What do you do when faced with a challenging situation, a question completely off topic, an attendee that wants to dominate the session or worse someone who is simply being nasty?

As a speaker you do not want to get into an argument or a heated debate with an audience member. You want to demonstrate professionalism and class while managing the difficult situation. This can be difficult when you feel like you are under attack, however you are in the position of authority while on the stage, so listen to the question or comment being put forward and think about how you can use this to make a positive point or learning for all.

When responding, first thank the person, by name preferably, then rephrase the question. This technique allows you time to think about your answer and how to provide a value-add response.

If there is somebody that is being a bit of a challenge and all their questions are off topic, negative or require an in-depth response, you may want to respectfully put a hold to the questions and offer to speak to them privately after the session or set-up a time to discuss.

Here are some of my go to responses to help me with difficult situations:

- Thank you, Danny, if I understand right, the question is ...

- Thank you, Lola, that is a great question, I feel it would be better for us to discuss one-on-one after the presentation.

- Thank you, Barkley, I'm hearing ..., I appreciate your point of view, from my experience ...

- Thank you, Taj, I'm not clear how this relates to the topic, what am I missing?

- Thank you, Molly, this is important therefore I would like to park these questions for now and we can discuss in private after the session today.

- Thank you, Maggie, I do not have the time to fully explore this with you now, let's catch-up to discuss after the session.

I believe by being prepared, it helps you to remain calm and in control when faced with difficult situations. Stay true to yourself and your content.

Setting up the Q & A

Let the audience know during your opening if there will be an opportunity for Q & A and when it will be. A simple statement like:

- And before I conclude my presentation today, we will have 5 minutes for questions.

In doing that, you are letting the audience know there will be opportunity for them to speak towards the end and that you will then bring them back for the conclusion.

When you reach the point in your presentation for the Q & A, it is important to set-up the session properly. By providing clear instructions at the start of the session, you will set the tone for the session and it will help you maintain control.

When considering how you want to manage the Q & A session you need to be specific. Use these questions to help you identify how you want to manage your session:

- How do you want the audience members to identify that they have a question? Should they raise their hand? Or if a small group, can they just ask their question?

- Would it help if they stood so you can see them clearly or can they remain seated?

- If in a large group, will they need to wait for a microphone before they ask their question?

- Do you want them to say their name first?

The benefit of asking their name is that you can address them personally when responding to their question. In the event, where there is hostility or a challenging situation, you can diffuse the situation simply by using their name. When you address the person by name, they are more inclined to soften their approach towards you.

I recommend that the set-up include:

- The length of the Q & A session either by time or number of questions.

- Remind them that after the Q & A you will conclude your presentation.

- Any specific instructions; raise your hand, state your name, wait for the microphone.

Here is an example of how I set-up a Q & A session:

> Now we have 10-minutes for questions before I share my final story. Please raise your hand to let me know you have a question. When I come to you, please let me know your name then ask your question. Where would you like to start?

Working the room

Having set clear instructions on how the Q & A session will run, you need to remember and follow your own instructions.

It is a good practice to repeat or rephrase questions each time as sometimes not everyone will hear the question. By repeating or rephrasing the question those that missed the original question will hear it when you say it.

When leading the Q & A session, try to involve the whole audience. This does not mean fielding a question from all attendees, but rather fielding questions from all parts of the room. Be mindful of where the questions are coming from and look to other parts of the room to field the next question.

One technique is to draw the attention to the parts of the room that are quiet:

- "I haven't heard from the people at the back, I'm going to take this question, then I'm heading your way."

- "It is very quiet over there, let's change that after this question."

If you get a response from a previously quiet area, wonderful, if you do not, they at least know that you cared enough to give them the opportunity to ask a question.

If you find that the session is being dominated by one or two people, you may want to consider the following at the end of your response:

- "Now let's see if somebody else has a question?"

- "Can I get a question from someone at the front (or back) of the room?"

- "Let's hear from someone that has not spoken today?"

When you are nearing the end of your allocated Q & A session, let the audience know that you have time for one more question before you conclude the presentation.

Finally, how will you close the Q & A session? I personally like to acknowledge the calibre of questions asked and the audience participation in the session. If there were people with unanswered questions, this is where you can advise how they can connect with you if they have further questions.

Action: Decide if you will include a Q & A session or not.

When considering if you will or won't have a Q & A session ask yourself the following:

- Will having a Q & A add value to my presentation and audience engagement?

- Will the audience want to ask questions and share their thoughts?

- If I don't have a Q & A, how can audience members connect with me if they have questions or want more information?

Action: Prepare for your Q & A session.

To prepare for your Q & A session complete the following:

1. Brainstorm potential questions.

2. Identify which questions need to be answered in the presentation.

3. For the remaining questions, prepare short to the point answers and practice them.

4. Think about how you will manage silence, no questions.

5. Decide what you will do when you do not know the answer.

6. If faced with a difficult situation, how do you plan to handle it?

7. How long will you have for the Q & A session?

8. What will you say to let the attendees know that there will be a Q & A later in the presentation?

9. How will you introduce the Q & A session? What instructions will you give the attendees?

10. How do you plan to work the room?

11. How will you close the Q & A session?

A final word on to Q & A or not

You do not need to fear a Q & A session. Questions asked by the audience members can provide valuable insight as to how your message is being received. Be prepared and you will facilitate a successful Q & A session.

Speaking It's NOT Worse Than Death

CHAPTER 6

The Bookends Matter

> Starting strong is good. Finishing strong is epic.
> **ROBIN SHARMA**

With the fear of speaking overshadowing me, I dreaded the beginning of my speech. Making the first contact with the audience as I said my opening lines, my mind was racing, will they like me, will they like what I have to say? It was all about me, my fear and my nerves. The conclusion of my speech was something I looked forward to because it meant that I was done, it was finished, the end. I could escape and collapse in my own private space and forget all about the speech. Back then it was all about me.

Over time, my fear dissolved and I grew more confident as a speaker. I began to appreciate that my speech was more about the audience than me. As a result, my thoughts on the opening of the speech changed from a place of fear to an opportunity to connect. The conclusion was still something I looked forward to, however now for a different reason. I saw it as the last opportunity for me to drive home my message and to leave something for the audience to remember.

The opening and conclusion are the bookends for your speech. They both have important roles to ensure that your message connects with the audience.

During this chapter you will:

- unlock the keys to opening to connect, and
- drive home your overall message with a conclusion to be remembered.

Open to connect

You may have heard "first impressions count", and in speeches they certainly do. With your opening you want to hook the audience from the start, you want to connect with them and have them eager to hear what you have to say.

From my experience it takes approximately 7 to 15 seconds for the audience members to warm to you. In the first 15 to 45 seconds of your speech the audience members are deciding if they what to hear what you have to say or if they will switch on their phone and read their emails, or worse, leave. Don't waste a second of the opportunity to make a great first impression. Use your time wisely and look at your opening from the attendees' place in audience and not your place on stage.

When you connect with your audience from the start, your fear of speaking lessens. Any nervousness will settle as you will be in the moment with the audience. Seeing the audience members smiling and nodding their heads within the opening of your speech will boost your confidence and make your feel more comfortable.

When you feel that connection with your audience, you are not alone on the stage, you feel safe, and you are able to speak more confidently.

If you don't connect with the audience in your opening, it will be harder to connect with them during your speech. Delivering your speech without connecting with your audience will heighten your nervousness and increase your fear of speaking.

Creating your opening

In the first moments of a speech, you want to connect with the audience, you want to let them know why they need to hear your speech and you want to give them the roadmap so they can follow your speech.

To connect with the audience immediately, you want to be different to other speakers. You want to avoid "good evening ladies and gentlemen, I am happy to be here today," or "good morning, thank you for having me." They aren't engaging. If you want to acknowledge the audience be creative and weave it into the opening but don't have it as the first words out of your mouth.

The first words out of your mouth need to instantly engage the audience, grab their attention. Here are three ways to connect with your audience from the moment you begin your speech:

- you can open with a story

- you can pose a thought-provoking question, or

- you can shock with a startling statement.

An opening story that sets up the reason for your speech. As mentioned in the 'unlock your story' chapter, people love stories, they relate to them and therefore they connect.

> "The fear of public speaking used to consume me. Speaking in front of groups. Groups of two or more used to fill me with dread. My heart would accelerate, I felt ill in the stomach and if you were there you would have seen me shaking as my face turned red..."

A thought-provoking question can take your audience to a place where they will want to hear your speech.

> "What could you achieve if you were not afraid of public speaking?"

Opening with a startling statement will spark the audiences' interest.

> "You would rather die than give a speech."

Once you have connected with the audience, you then want to let them know why they need to listen to your speech and why they need to listen now. Be clear as to the value they will gain from your speech, and what is in it for them. I like to combine this with the roadmap that is created earlier in chapter 3, 'The Right Package'. The roadmap lets the audience know where you will be taking them during your speech.

> "In the next 20 minutes, you will collect 3 keys to unlock your fear of public speaking. With the **why key**, you will close the door on your fear. The **what key** opens the door to developing your speech and finally the **how key** will take you to the stage."

You want to move smoothly from your opening to your first main point with a transition statement.

> "With these keys in your pocket you will shut the door on your fear of speaking. Are you ready to lock the door on your fear?"

If you will be including a Q & A session, you will want to let the audience know before you move to your first point.

"I will then open the door for questions before wrapping up and closing. Are you ready to lock the door on your fear?"

If you want to acknowledge the audience try this:

"In the next 20 minutes, ladies and gentlemen, you will collect 3 keys to unlock your fear of public speaking."

Special acknowledgements

As a speaker in Australia, there have been times where I have acknowledged the traditional land owners before beginning my presentation. It is a sign of respect – all speakers presenting in a government building or at a government hosted event in Australia will firstly acknowledge the traditional land owners.

If speaking in other locations, I suggest you check with the event organisers to see if there is a local acknowledgement.

When doing an acknowledgement, ensure that you have the correct wording. Practice saying it before the event. After the acknowledgement allow a short pause, before launching into your opening.

Conclude to be remembered

Your conclusion is the last thing the audience will hear you say. You want to drive home your overall message – that way if the audience remembers nothing else from your speech, they will at least remember your last words. Your final words count! Make them memorable.

Having taken the audience members on a journey, you want to pull it together, leaving the audience with no doubt as to the overall message and the value added for them.

When you finish strong, you will walk off the stage feeling confident, knowing that you have connected with the audience and that your overall message has been received.

Creating your conclusion

In the conclusion you do not want to just repeat your main points, you want to drive home the overall message. Show the audience how the main points, when packaged together, arrive at the overall message. As you do this you are reminding the audience of each of the three main points, further securing a place in their memory. You want to encourage the attendees to not just hear your message but to apply the lessons and reap the benefits.

I find concluding your speech with a story is an effective tool to anchor your overall message – a story that illustrates the main points coming together to culminate in the overall message. If your overall message is for the audience to think or do something different, then recapping the main points within a story seems less like a shopping list and more achievable. If your overall message is for the audience to feel something, using a story to highlight the feeling will connect better than just telling them to feel a particular way.

Building your speech to a memorable conclusion will leave you on a high as you finish your speech. This will fill you with confidence and you will be less fearful of speaking.

In my early days as a speaker, I always concluded my speeches by thanking the audience. I thought it was polite to do so, as they had taken the time to listen to me and I was grateful they had. What I hadn't realised was that after wrapping up my speech, the last thing the audience heard was, "thank you, thank you very much". It worked for Elvis but it doesn't work for you as a speaker. You want the last words to be your overall message. You do not need to thank the audience, the audience will thank you by their applause, because you have taken the time to speak to them, to share your message. Accept their thanks graciously, acknowledge it with a nod or a smile. You do not need to say thank you. If thanking the audience is important to you, find a way to weave in the thank you before you deliver your final line.

As part of your conclusion, you may want to offer a product or service at a special rate. If you do, I recommend that you reference the product or service during your speech. As a coach, I may reference a coaching client when making a point or highlight a coaching resource during my speech. When I do this, I am planting the seed for the offer. I often share my own focus on continued learning and investing in my own professional development, planting more seeds for the offer at the end. I'm not going to fill my speech with "I'm a coach, I'm a coach," as that would be annoying and devalue the content and me as a coach. There must be value in the speech for the audience, it cannot be just a sales pitch. Where the opportunity arises to plant the seed, use it, but never overuse it. The benefit of planting the seed is that when I come to promoting my coaching services, the audience is already aware of the service and have an insight on the benefits of the service. As a speaker and an audience member I am more comfortable with this soft sell approach.

When you introduce the special offer, be clear on what the offer is.

Here is how I may wrap up my presentation:

> My life changed when I began to break down the walls of my fear. With commitment and determination, I gained confidence by opening the door to develop my public speaking skills. I now actively look for opportunities to speak and continue to develop my skills. When you face your fear armed with the right tools anything is possible. As a thank you for warmly welcoming me here, for today only, I am offering my standard coaching package at a 15% discount, plus a signed copy of my book "Speaking, It's NOT Worse Than Death" and a recording of this presentation. Join me at the back of the room after this session to secure your package. Don't let the fear of speaking hold you back any more. Face your fear, open the door and let the world know you have something to say.

Action: Develop your opening.

Use these 5 steps to create your opening:

1. How can you gain the audiences interest and attention within the first 15 seconds? What will be the first words you say?

2. Why should the audience listen to your speech? What is in it for them?

3. How will you introduce your roadmap?

4. If you decided to have a Q & A, how will you let the audience know?

5. How will you transition to your first main point?

Action: Develop your conclusion.

Use these 3 steps to create your conclusion:

1. How will you wrap up your speech and drive home your main point?

2. Will you include a special offer?

3. What will be the final words you say?

Action: Add your opening and conclusion to your speech.

Write your opening and conclusion.

Use your transition statement to link to the first main point.

Use the transition statement from your third main point to link to the conclusion.

Your first draft of your speech will be complete with an opening, 3 main points, conclusion and transition statements.

A final word on bookends matter

Your time in front of the audience is limited, therefore you must make the most of every second. Use your time wisely. Engage with the audience from your first words and make your final words memorable.

Speaking It's NOT Worse Than Death

CHAPTER 7

Using Your Voice

Words mean more than what is set down on paper
It takes the human voice to infuse them with deeper meaning.
MAYA ANGELOU

You know what you are going to say but how will you say it?

A speaker who embraces their voice and provides variety will have me sitting up and listening to their every word.

From my experience nervous speakers will often speak softly and fast with little to no change in tone. It often seems like they have held their breath for the whole speech. It is like the nervousness is driving the speech rather than the speaker. When a speaker is too quiet, the audience will struggle to hear and the message will not be received.

When the speaker is speaking too fast, the audience will struggle to keep up and the message will be unclear.

As a speaker you want your message to be heard. Give your message a chance, find the right mix of tone, volume and pace to provide your audience with an enjoyable listening experience.

During this chapter you will explore:

- how to incorporate vocal variety into your delivery, and
- activities and tips to help you develop your vocal variety.

Enhance your vocal variety

To enhance your vocal variety, you need to expand your voice and use:

- tone
- volume
- pace, and
- pause.

Tone

It pains me to sit through a presentation with a monotonous speaker. Whether they speak slow and low or fast and loud, the sameness is painful. From their first word to the last, the speaker uses the same tone, volume and pace. Whether it is a short or long presentation, the sameness will have me falling asleep or counting the seconds until the speaker is finished. For me, monotone screams boring!

A speech needs emotion. As an audience member I want to feel what the speaker is saying, and it is hard to do that when the speaker has no emotion and their delivery is monotonous.

When delivering your speech, if you are angry, be angry. If you are sad, be sad. If you are excited, be excited. When you feel the emotion through your voice, your audience will feel it too.

Varying your tone can be effective when delivering humorous content, especially when the emotions expressed contradict the words being said.

To help you get used to using different tones in your delivery, consider adding emojis to your notes to prompt you to use specific tones.

Look for opportunities to use different tones to add impact and interest to your speech.

Volume

As a speaker you want to be heard and depending on the size of the audience you may need to adjust your normal speaking volume. In smaller groups or when using a microphone, I will use my normal speaking voice volume, the one I use when I am at home. When speaking in a larger group without a microphone, I need to lift the volume of my normal speaking voice to be able to reach the back of the room.

In addition to your normal speaking volume, you may use softer or louder volumes throughout your speech. Your softer volume needs to be heard by all, not just those in the front row. With your louder volume be mindful not to deafen those in the front row. Adjusting your normal speaking volume when in a larger room will ensure that you can still use soft and loud volumes.

I am not a quiet speaker naturally, therefore using my normal speaking voice, with a softer and louder volume, works for me.

If your natural speaking voice volume is soft, there is a risk that your soft volume voice will be unheard. Therefore, I recommend you focus on introducing two louder speaking voices, one for your normal speaking voice and one for your louder volume voice. Your natural speaking volume can be used for your soft voice when delivering your speech.

Where you are a naturally loud speaker, there is a risk that your loud volume voice will come across as though you are yelling. Therefore, I recommend you focus on introducing two softer speaking voices, one for a normal speaking voice and one for your soft volume voice. Your natural speaking volume can be used for the loud voice during your speech.

Before the event starts, I recommend you test your volume by enlisting the help of one of the organisers. Agree on signals they can use in the practice and during the speech to let you know to increase or decrease your volume. Test your normal voice, soft voice and loud voice. Never be afraid to enlist the help of others.

Use your soft and loud volumes to emphasise words and phrases during your speech. Using your loud volume for emphasis can be like a jolt, whereas using the soft volume can draw the audience in. Both provide a sit up and listen moment for the audience.

To practice using volume read a sentence and use volume to stress specific words. I find this particularly useful as it shows you how you can change the meaning of the sentence just by emphasising a particular word.

To help you get used to using different volumes in your delivery, consider adding up and down arrows to your notes as a prompt for when to change your volume. Alternatively, you could **BOLD AND CAPITAL FOR LOUD** and *italics lower case for soft*.

Pace

When you fear speaking, your focus is often on the end of the speech and getting there as quick as you can. As a result, you race through your speech, possibly forgetting to breathe. When you finish, you suck in a deep breath and let go a sigh of relief. You did it, you finished, you made it to the end. While you are feeling good having finished the race, the audience is still at the starting line wondering what happened. While speed does have a place in a speech, you do not want to run the race on your own.

Like with volume, you want to have a normal speaking pace plus a fast and slow pace. To reach the fast or slow place, at different times you may jump straight to it or escalate to it.

If you are looking to create excitement, increase the rate of your speech instantly or gradually. I find there is a natural link to my personal excitement and the rate of my speech. Pace can be effective in creating feelings, like confusion. To demonstrate confusion within your speech, you may rapidly share your thoughts, increasing the pace as you do so, until you're out of breath and stop to take a deep breath. This can create a sense of confusion, heightened anxiety and helps your audience to not just listen to your words but to feel them too.

Slowing your pace to add emphasis to a particular word or phrase will have the audience hanging on to your every word. Mixing up the pace will keep it interesting for the audience.

To help you get used to using different rates of speech in your delivery, consider using a red bold to prompt you to speak faster and s p a c e   o u t   y o u r   w o r d s when you want to speak slower.

Pause

Pauses allow the audience to reflect and stay connected during the speech. There is a lost opportunity when a speaker poses a powerful, thought provoking question to the audience and continues without a pause. While the speaker may not want the audience to yell out the answer, they do want them to answer the questions, therefore they should pause and allow them time to do so.

Pauses help slow down the pace of your speech, allowing the audience to keep up with the speaker. When you have an important point to make, taking a short pause will allow the audience to be with you and be ready to receive the point.

The length of a pause required in your speech will vary depending on the purpose of the pause. If it is to allow the audience time to think and come up with an answer to a powerful question, the pause would need to be longer than if the question was closed, requiring a yes or no answer.

A joke or humorous line that does not hit the mark is awkward. Using a well-placed pause can be the difference between a joke or humorous line being funny or a flop. Use the pause to add anticipation, then hit them with the punch line. Do not over extend the pause as it can then become ineffective. Practice telling jokes, to family and friends, using different length pauses before the punch lines. Take note of punch lines that hit the mark and those that are less effective – notice the length of the pauses. Creating an awareness of use of pauses and practicing telling jokes will help you when you have a humorous line to deliver in your speech.

Where your audience is enjoying a laugh, take a pause and let them laugh. If you cut their laughter short, it can impact the audience laughing at other humorous lines. They may still laugh however it is likely to be more restrained because you cut them off once, and they will be expecting you to do it again.

Bringing characters to life

Stories provide an opportunity to introduce vocal variety through your characters dialogue. You do not need to be a Robin Williams to bring your characters to life, you can use tone, volume and pace. There are many combinations to consider. For a child talking about their holiday you might use soft, fast with an overall excited tone. Try different combinations until you find one that will work for your character.

Reading children's story books out-loud is a technique to help bring characters to life. There is something about the magic of a children's book that opens us up to using our vocal variety.

Action: Develop your vocal variety.

Use the following activities to help you develop your vocal variety. For best value, I recommend you record yourself and then listen to the recording.

Tone

Say the following sentence seven times, expressing a different emotion each time:

Tomorrow is Monday.

1. Joy.

2. Excitement.

3. Surprise.

4. Anger.

5. Fear.

6. Sadness.

7. Disgust.

Notice how your tone changes with the different emotions.

Continue to practice expressing your emotions using different sentences.

Volume

Say the following sentence seven times, and as you do this stress the **bold** word only:

I didn't say we should sign-up today.

I **didn't** say we should sign-up today.

I didn't **say** we should sign-up today.

I didn't say **we** should sign-up today.

I didn't say we **should** sign-up today.

I didn't say we should **sign-up** today.

I didn't say we should sign-up **today**.

Notice how the meaning of a sentence changes as you emphasise different words.

Continue to practice using volume to emphasise words and phrases.

Pace and pauses

To practice your pace and speaking with pauses, read out-loud a piece from this book or another book, or from a newspaper or online article.

Use a different pace for each sentence, followed by a pause.

Paces to use:

- fast pace for full sentence
- slow pace for full sentence
- normal pace for full sentence
- fast pace becoming slower
- slow pace becoming faster

Vary the length of the pauses. Firstly, pause for a count of 3. Just say in your mind 1, 2, 3.

Then pause for longer, a count of 5 and a count of 10.

Notice the impact that pace and pauses make to the delivery.

Continue to practice using pace and pauses.

Characters

Using tone, volume, pace and pauses create voices for at least two characters.

Listen to the recording to see if you can clearly identify the different characters by the voice you created.

Try different combinations of tone, volume, pace and pauses to find the right character voices for your speech.

Action: Add vocal variety to your speech.

Record yourself practicing your speech.

Listen to the recording and highlight where you effectively used different tones, volume, pace and pauses.

- Did you emphasise the right words and phrases?
- Were you speaking soft or loud?
- Are you able to clearly identify the voices of your characters?
- Were your pauses long enough for the audience to answer the question, or to catch-up and take a breath?
- Where could you add more vocal variety?

A final word on using your voice

Stretch your vocal variety by playing around with your tone, volume and pace. Record yourself every opportunity you can and notice where you are using your voice effectively and where you can improve.

As a speaker, it is not just what you say that counts, but how you say it.

CHAPTER 8

Make a Move

Words represent your intellect.
The sound, gesture and movement represent your feelings.
PATRICIA FRIPP

Utilising the stage area and your body with purpose will help you engage with your audience and anchor your main points, while providing an outlet for any nervous energy.

Whether you are fixed to a lectern or have the freedom to work the stage, make movement part of your presentation.

During this chapter you will uncover how to add impact to your speech using:

- facial expressions

- body movement, and

- the stage.

Facial expressions

Your face is a powerful tool. Connecting the emotion of your content with your facial gestures will enhance the emotion and the feeling for you and the audience.

I have witnessed speakers talking about death with a huge smile on their face. The content was sad and upsetting, yet they were beaming. The gesture did not match the content and the speaker came across as unauthentic. I have seen nervous speakers talking about what sounds like exciting and happy times, with fear all over their face. It is hard for the audience to connect with the excitement and happiness when the speaker looks frightened.

Deliberately using the wrong facial gesture, however, can be used effectively to add humour to your presentation. The humour comes from the mixed message.

If you are nervous about giving your speech, consciously put on a smile as you stand to walk to the stage. The simple act of putting a smile on my face makes me feel more confident.

Do you know what your happy face, angry face and confused face looks like? A simple way to find out is to make faces in front of a mirror. Alternatively, you can take selfies making different faces then put an emotion to each of the photos.

The more you live your speech the more natural your facial gestures will be.

Body movement

Body movements can add impact to your speech or they can detract from your speech.

Overuse of particular gestures can be distracting for the audience and draw their attention away from your words, your message. Here are some of my distracting movements:

- playing with my hair or my earrings
- fiddling with my sleeve
- holding a pen, and worse, clicking the pen
- punctuating every word with a hand gesture
- licking my lips
- clasping hands, and
- shifting from foot to foot, or swaying.

I was unaware of these distracting movements until they were brought to my attention. Awareness is the first step to removing distracting gestures. Learning how to use body movement effectively, using purposeful movements and practicing will reduces any unwanted gestures.

Do you have any distracting gestures? If you are unsure, ask for feedback or record your presentations.

As a nervous speaker, I used to slouch, I was not confident and it showed. Be mindful of your posture when speaking. Stand tall with confidence.

Varying your posture can be an effective tool to differentiate between characters. One character could have a bit of a slouch, the other might be more laid back. You may want to show one character smaller than the other, and posture is a way to show the height difference. The shorter character may lean back slightly and look up at the other character to create a height difference. The tall character may stand tall and tilt their head as they look down at the other character.

When thinking of body movement think whole body, arms, legs, head. If you are fixed to a lectern then you will predominately use your upper body, however, I have seen a speaker lift their leg to the side to show off their shoe to make a point. Body movement can be anything from a simple nod of the head or a wink to acting out a movement, like hitting a ball.

Body movement exaggeration is an effective tool to add humour to the presentation. Exaggerating on size can be effective. Using body movement to deliberately contradict your words can create humour, for example: saying the person was huge, they were so big, then using your hand to show they were actually shorter than you.

Body movement may need to be adjusted depending on the size of the audience. A small movement may be lost if the audience is large. A large movement may be overpowering if the audience is small. A wink could be lost in a large room, unless the presentation is being projected onto large screens.

The more you practice using body movements, the more natural they will become.

Nervous body movements

Sometimes when we are nervous, our body does things that increases our stress in the moment. I recall standing on the stage in Kuala Lumpur in front of hundreds of people, and my right knee started to shake uncontrollably. Fortunately, I was wearing a skirt, past my knee, so no-one could see the shaking. As my knee was shaking my stress levels grew, until I scrunched my toes, then released them before lifting my heal slightly off the ground and pushing my big toe into the stage. That small movement unseen by the audience anchored me and stopped the knee from shaking.

While delivering the eulogy at my dad's celebration of life, my emotions started to surface and my right hand started to shake. To stop the shakes, I pressed the tip of my ring finger and my thumb together until the shakes eased. This was again unseen by the audience but was an effective use of body movement.

My learning from both of these experiences was to first acknowledge the situation, then do something about it. I feel the act of doing something is the key, and not necessarily what I did.

Using the stage

Whether you have the freedom to move across the stage or are restricted to the lectern, you can use the stage to add impact to your message.

Freedom to move

Where you have the freedom to move across the stage or the stage area, make the most of it. Using the stage to anchor your main points allows the audience to connect that section of the stage with the point – it helps them to recall the different parts of your speech easier.

One technique is to use the stage as your presentation timeline, taking your audience on a journey across the stage from one side to the other as you progress through your main points.

When I use the stage as a presentation timeline, I begin on my right, the audience's stage left, with my first point. I read from left to write, therefore when I am following someone on stage, it flows naturally for me when they start on stage left, move to centre stage and then deliver their final point stage right. When considering staging think about the audience and how will it feel for them watching. You want your speech to provide a logical flow from the audiences view point, not yours.

The presentation timeline can be used for making your points in chronological order: point 1 to the left, point 2 in the centre and point 3 to the right. This works well for speeches with a past, present and future theme. The past is stage left, present is centre stage and future is stage right.

Another technique I have used when comparing two points of view is to place the two points of view on opposite sides of the stage, then move to centre stage when comparing the points. I deliver the first point stage left and the second point stage right, still using the left to right concept. When I am centre stage comparing the two points, I can gesture with my hand or head to the relevant side of the stage and instantly take the audience back to that point.

The stage provides the opportunity to anchor your stories. Depending on the stage area available, you may have three sections: stage left, centre stage and stage right. For a larger stage area, you may be able to section the stage more with front of stage and back of stage, creating six sections of stage, or for a larger area you may even be able to add middle stage to make nine sections. When on a large stage, if you use the back of the stage, be mindful that the further back you are, the harder it is to connect with the audience.

I recall a speaker named David who used the back of stage effectively in a speech competition. He started back of stage, in the centre, facing away from the audience. He began speaking in character, a superior in the Army. He painted the picture that the superior was looking out the window while he addressed the young soldier. I was hooked immediately; the opening was different and it made me sit up and listen. Throughout the speech, David simply looked or gestured to the back of stage and I was instantly transported back to the opening story. The speaker used a microphone so his voice was able to carry from the back of the stage to the audience. Without a microphone, he would have wanted to test his voice beforehand to ensure it was not lost when facing away from the audience.

When using the stage, be mindful of where you place your stories and the scene you create. If you dig a hole, or you put a lake or a pond in a scene, you do not want to find yourself falling in it later in your speech. I do not mean actually falling on stage, but I mean walking straight through the place where you previously had set that scene. You do not want the audience thinking "hang on, they just walked in the pond". If they do, the impact of the story and placement on stage is lost. To avoid this happening, place, large objects, holes, towards the side, middle or back of stage. Alternatively, you could place it off the stage. This way if you happen to forget where you placed the object or hole, you will not accidently bump into it or fall in as you walk across the front of the stage. Planning where you will anchor your stories and the scene you are painting will help you avoid any mishaps on stage.

Once you have anchored a story or main point to a section of the stage, you want to keep it in that place for the duration of your speech. This allows you to reference the point at other times and in your conclusion, a comment or a gesture of the hand or head can transport the audience back to the scene or the point. This means you do not need to restate the full story or point for the audience to connect with it. This is the power of anchoring your point, painting the scene – the audience will remember.

By planning how you will use the stage and where you will be when you deliver your main points, you are less likely to forget your content and this will reduce your nervousness during the presentation.

Nervous pacing

Pacing, when a speaker is moving back and forward across the stage area, is often seen as a nervous movement. Whether they are moving fast or ambling back and forth, the movement can be distracting for the audience. The audience is focused on watching you move rather than what you say. This is where using the stage can help. Decide before you walk on stage where you will be making your main points, how will you use movement during your speech. You want to move with purpose, while remaining natural. If you are a pacer on stage, you will want to consciously anchor yourself when you are not moving with purpose. The technique I shared before can help – scrunch your toes and then press them to the ground. It is hard to walk without stumbling when you do this, and as a result you will stand still.

From the lectern

When you are speaking from a lectern or a fixed microphone, you may still be able to utilise parts of the stage by using a gesture to anchor a point or story to a section of the stage. While using your hand to direct the audience to stage left, you say, "In the past", then when speaking about the future you gesture to stage right. Using effective hand gestures will help you set the scenes on stage.

Action: Add impact to your speech with facial gestures and body movement.

Use these questions to help you identify how you can use facial gestures and body movement to add impact to your speech.

- What emotions do I want to express during my speech?

- Will my facial gestures match the emotions or not?

- What gestures and body movement can I use to add impact to my speech?

- Will I need to adjust my gestures for the size of the audience?

To help develop your use of facial gestures and body movement, you might find it valuable to add notes to your draft speech to prompt you when practicing.

Action: Plan how you will use the stage.

Use these questions to help you plan your use of the stage.

- Where will I be on stage when I begin speaking?
- Where will I deliver my final words?
- Where will I place my first main point?
- Where will I place my second main point?
- Where will I place my third main point?
- What scenes will I be creating on stage?

Action: Record yourself practicing your speech.

Record yourself practicing your speech and when you watch the recording, look for how you are using movement.

- Are your facial gestures matching the emotion of your words?
- Are you effectively using your facial gestures to heighten the emotion?
- Do you have any distracting gestures?

- Are your gestures and body movement aligned with the words?

- Are you using the stage area as a timeline?

- Are you setting the scene for your stories?

Use your observations to make improvements to your delivery.

A final word on make a move

Effective use of gestures and stage will enhance the audiences experience. Planning how to use gestures and stage will give you focus during the presentation and help you to recall content.

Utilising the stage to drive home your message is a bonus. Without the flexibility of movement, your words need to be able to stand on their own and paint the picture to make the point.

CHAPTER 9

Selecting Your Accessories

Knowledge is always accompanied with
accessories of emotion and purpose.
ALFRED NORTH WHITEHEAD

Visual aids can enhance your speech but should never overshadow the speech. The speech has to be able to stand alone without visual aids. Visual aids can help you stay focused during your speech. Knowing you have a prop or slide show to keep you on topic can give you confidence and lessen your anxiety.

During this chapter you will explore using:

- props
- slide shows
- flip charts
- handouts, and
- notes.

Props

A well-used prop can help the audience connect with your message.

When thinking props, use the KISS principle: keep it simple and safe. The prop must add value to your speech, it must support a main point and help drive the message home. Props are optional – if you do want to use a prop, do so but don't over-complicate the speech by using a lot of props.

Here are some simple props that I have seen used successfully:

- Glass of red wine for a speech that was exploring the concept of half full or half empty.
- A seed, for a speech that was encouraging the idea that action begins with a single seed of an idea.
- A handbag filled with expected and unexpected items, used for a humorous speech highlighting that you never know what is inside a lady's handbag.
- A photo of a dog in an emotional speech about loss and companionship.

- Three bonsai plants, where each plant was used to illustrate a leadership lesson.

- A man in a suit, who removes the suit jacket and shirt to show a muscle top and tattoos, for his speech about not judging people by appearances.

As you can see props can be simple, and varied. The key is, will it add value to your speech or not? Will the prop help the audience connect with your main point, your story? Years later I can still remember the point of these props in the speech, therefore I believe the speakers chose well when they selected their props.

Beware of over using props or using props with no value. Don't have a prop just for the sake of having a prop.

I recall one speaker who wanted to put a green rug on the floor to represent grass. The problem was the audience was large and only those in the front row would have seen the rug. Using the rug added no value to the speech. Now if the speaker was speaking in an auditorium with raised seating, then this prop could have been effective.

Lots of props may be difficult to manage and may be confusing for the audience. As a general rule less is more when you think of props. One effective prop is better than many ineffective props.

Using many props can be memorable with the right props and practice. Australian Bush Poet Gregory North uses a chest full of hats for his rendition of Banjo Paterson's 'The Man From Snowy River'. Each hat represents a different character and Greg nails it every time I see him present. Just thinking of it brings a smile to my face.

If you do decide to use a lot of props, make sure they add value, can be seen by the audience and that you practice, practice, practice using them.

Selecting a prop

When thinking about using a prop ask yourself these questions:

- What prop can be used to illustrate the main point?
- Will the prop be used, shown or worn?
- Will the prop help the audience to connect with the main point?
- Will the prop be easy for the audience to see?
- Will the prop be easy to set-up and pack-up?
- Can you set-up and pack-up the prop yourself or will you need help?
- Will extra equipment be required to display the prop?

Using the prop

Once you have selected your prop, you need to consider the following:

- When will the prop be introduced?
- How will you introduce and use the prop?
- How long will the prop be used for?
- What will you do with the prop when it is no longer needed?

When a prop is introduced depends on the prop, the content and value it brings. There may be times when a prop can be displayed for the duration of the speech, while other times, it may be better for the prop to be hidden until the appropriate time. After using the prop, only keep it visible if it will continue to add value, as a reminder for the audience or if you will refer to it later. If you are not going to use it again, remove it from sight as you do not want the prop to take the focus away from you and your content.

When practicing your speech, practice with your prop. Practice setting up the prop, using the prop and packing up the prop. All aspects of using the prop need to be practiced. You do not want to fumble with the prop during the speech as it will lose impact and may trigger your nerves.

If you are one of many speakers at the event, you will want to ensure you can easily get the prop on and off stage without too much disruption, and without impacting other speakers.

Slide shows

Using a slide show is a useful tool to help you as a speaker stay on topic.

The use of a slide show is the most common visual aid used by speakers. When using slides, apply the KISS principal again: keep it simple and short.

Your presentation must be able to stand on its own without the slides. Therefore, you need to prepare your presentation first, then design your slides. Keep your slides to a minimum if you are doing a 10-minute presentation, I would suggest no more than four slides, however as few as one slide could work. Like props, slides must add value to your presentation.

When thinking about using a slide show ask yourself these questions:

- How will using a slide show add value to the presentation?
- How many slides will I use?

- Does the venue have facilities for a slide show?
- Will you need to use your own device or the venues?

When designing your slide think less is more. Here are my tips for designing your slides:

- A single image or statement is more effective than a slide of dot points.
- Be consistent with your branding on your slides.
- Text should be easy to read.
- Use bold colours as they are easier to see.
- Avoid colour background and colour text together as it can be difficult for people with colour blindness to see.
- Limit the type of transitions used. Just because the software provides them, doesn't mean you have to use them all.
- If embedding a video or audio track into the slide show, have a back-up in case the presentation freezes.

Before the event practice delivering your presentation with your slides. Here are some slide show tips:

- Invest in a wireless presenter device.
    - Using the device will allow you to move away from the computer during the presentation.
    - Practice using the device, moving to next slide, going back to previous slide and blacking the screen.

- o Take spare batteries and have them in your pocket or near the stage, so you can easily grab them if needed during the presentation.

- Test the slide show on arrival at the venue.

    - o Have the slide show on your own device and on a USB.

    - o Ensure your device is fully charged, in case you cannot use the power cord.

    - o Take an extension cord.

    - o Use your wireless presenter device when testing the slide show.

- Avoid walking in front of the screen – instead, stand to the side. If you want to move to the other side, then black the screen first. You do not want to be blinded by the projectors light.

- If you choose to use dot points, avoid reading from the screen word for word. If you want to see what is on the screen, set-up your device in front of you on the stage. This way you can see what is on the screen without turning your back to the audience.

- If you do want the audience to read what is on the screen, turn to the screen and read. This will prompt the audience to follow your lead and read the screen.

- Only display slides when needed, and black the screen the rest of the time. If you leave the slide on the screen audience members will keep being drawn back to it. Therefore, only keep the slide up if it is adding value.

- If you are running out of time, consider blacking the screen and not using slides. Flicking through slides and skipping over content because you are running out of time leaves the audience feeling like they are missing out on something.

The big risk when using a slide show is that it does not work. If technology does not work or plays up on the day, you still need to be able to deliver your speech without the slides. Your speech needs to be able to stand on its own because you never know when technology will fail.

Flip charts

Flip charts and whiteboards can come in handy and, with them, you do not need to worry about technology failing.

Flip charts can be prepared earlier or left blank and used in the moment. You could use a flip chart for an activity and note the audiences answers.

Here are my tips for using a flip chart:

- Use colours that can be seen from the back of the room. Avoid green – I find it difficult to see unless up close.

- When preparing your flip chart, print clearly and ensure no spelling mistakes.

- Leave the first page blank, so that you can use it to hide the content when it is not required.

- If you want to remove the page and display on wall, I recommend using a post-it note style of flip charter otherwise you will need to take tape or tac to fix it to the wall. Check with venue before using tape or tac.

- Consider engaging a helper to act as scribe for activities where audience members responses are to be recorded. This allows you to maintain the connection with the audience during the activity.

If using a whiteboard, ensure you are using whiteboard markers, not permanent markers, and use a clean whiteboard eraser. If you want to hide what is on the board during the presentation, turn the whiteboard around.

Handouts

To support your message, you may elect to use handouts.

Design your handout after you have created your speech content. Like the content in your speech, the handout must directly support your main points and overall message.

As you design your handout consider when and how it will be provided to the attendees:

- by email prior to or after the event

- as they arrive or placed on their seat ready for them to arrive

- at a set time during your speech, or

- at the end of the speech.

Providing a handout prior to the event provides the opportunity for attendees to read material before they arrive. This is useful if you want them to have specific knowledge before your speech.

When training Toastmasters Club Executive Officers, I would email them the link to the Club Officer Leadership manual and encourage them to read it before they attended training. By doing this the attendees, at a minimum, should have an understanding of their role and the team's roles when they arrive.

Not everyone will do the pre-reading, therefore you can't assume they have. The best way I have found to manage this is to include a debrief activity related to the pre-reading content.

Providing handouts prior the event is good for attendees who wish to save paper, as they can download the material onto their devices.

I have found providing handouts prior to the event extremely useful for attendees who are vision impaired, as they can use their text to voice software to read the handouts. A tip for making your documents accessible for vision impaired is to use the Check Accessibility function in Microsoft Word.

Providing handouts on arrival gives those that arrive early something to read while they wait for the start. They also know that they do not have to take loads of notes as you have given them key information already. You may elect to have attendees collect the handout when they sign-in at the registration desk. This is the easiest way to distribute the handout, especially for large groups. An alternate method is to place the handout on seats in the room before attendees arrive.

Providing handouts during the speech works when you want the audience to arrive at the same point together. To do this you will need to consider how you distribute the handout. In a small group you may decide to walk around the room distributing the handout as you are speaking. Alternatively, you may wish to give handouts to one person and ask them to take one and pass them on. Another option is to engage the help of others to distribute the handouts. If engaging the help of others, I recommend you set this up before you start. This is where the event organiser may be able to help identify helpers.

Providing handouts after the speech allows the audience to fully focus on you and your content. To do this you need to consider how the attendees can collect the handout. Will someone be standing at the door distributing the handout? Do they have to collect the handout from a table at the back of the room? Will you email the handout to them?

When you will distribute the handout determines the type of information you will include in the handout. If providing the handout prior to, on arrival or during the speech, the handout may be a worksheet where the attendees fill-in answers throughout the speech. I like worksheet handouts as it provides the attendees with something to do during the speech. You can simply use headings with space for attendees to write their thoughts, or you can instruct them on what to write. I like to use fill-in the blank on my handouts, as the attendees are more inclined to listen to what I am saying so they don't miss out on what to write in the blank. The completed handout becomes a resource of the main points. If using a worksheet handout, ensure that attendees are asked to bring a pen with them to the event or you provide pens.

Handouts provided prior to or after the speech may include additional reading on the topic. I recommend that you avoid having additional reading in handouts provided on arrival and during the speech. If you do, the attendees may focus on reading the handout rather than listening to you.

When providing handouts confirm with the event coordinator beforehand the number of attendees and ensure you have enough copies and extras.

Make sure that you use good quality paper and that the print is clear. If asking attendees to print the handouts, consider how much colour you have on the handout. I recently printed a handout that had a full page of blue background on the first and last page, and while it looked good on the screen, it used up a lot of my ink. This can be annoying for attendees, so limit your use of full-page colour in handouts when asking attendees to print.

Using notes

For most speeches, following the structure provided in this book and with practice will mean you should not need to use notes. However, there are times where notes or a full script is needed. For most of my speeches I use no notes, however for eulogies I always use a full script.

Notes should be brief, and used to trigger your memory. When using notes, I suggest:

- Keep it simple and on a single page.
    - Two pages can work but print them single sided and have them side by side on the lectern.
    - Number your pages.
- Use large font. The font should be easily read from a standing position, if you drop the page on the floor. This will make it easy for you to glance at the notes during your presentation. I used to recommend Arial 22 point however as my eyes are getting old, this does not work for me. Find the font size that works best for you.
- Keep your notes brief:
    - Opening words.
    - Main points.
    - Sub points.
    - Closing words.

Here are my tips for using a full script:

- Use large font, same as with notes.

- Use double spacing or 1 ½ spacing.

- Start each sentence on a new line.

- Add an extra line between paragraphs.

- Number your pages.

- Print single sided.

- Place all pages on the right-hand side of the lectern.

- As you near the end of the page, slowly move the page to the left. Doing this will allow you to move to the top of the next page easily.

- As you read your speech, lift your eyes regularly to make contact with the audience.

- Use your finger as a guide – this will help you easily find your place when your eyes return to the script.

- Practice reading the speech and lifting your eyes. If you can do it in front of a mirror, do so, as this way you can lift your eyes, make eye contact with yourself, before looking back at the script. The more you practice the easier it will be to read the script and make eye contact with the audience.

Action: Select your accessories

Use these questions to help you decide if you will use visual aids.

- Will a visual aid add value to the presentation?

- What type of visual aid will work best?

If using a prop:

- What prop can be used to illustrate the main point?
- Will the prop be used, shown or worn?
- Will the prop help the audience to connect with the main point?
- Will the prop be easy for the audience to see?
- Will the prop be easy to set-up and pack-up?
- Can you set-up and pack-up the prop yourself or will you need help?
- Will extra equipment be required to display the prop?
- When will the prop be introduced?
- How will you introduce and use the prop?
- How long will the prop be used?
- What will you do with the prop when it is no longer needed?

If using a slide show:

- How will using a slide show add value to the presentation?
- How many slides will I need?
- Does the venue have facilities for a slide show?
- Will I need to use my device or the venue's?

If using a flip chart:

- How will I use the flip chart?

- Will I prepare the pages beforehand?

If using handouts:

- When will the handouts be distributed?

- Will the handouts provide additional reading material or be a worksheet?

If using notes:

- Will I be using notes or a full script?

A final word on selecting your accessories

Only use a visual aid if it will add value to your speech and help the audience connect with your message, your main points. Your speech is the star of the show and the visual aids are the supporting actors. The show must go on if the visual aids do not work.

Speaking It's NOT Worse Than Death

CHAPTER 10

Let's Get Social

Courage starts with showing up
and letting ourselves be seen.
BRENE BROWN

Your role as a speaker starts on arrival at the venue and extends until you leave.

Networking is not one of my strengths - I'm socially awkward. It still gives me butterflies in my tummy when I attend networking events. However, when I am attending an event as a speaker, I am less nervous, more comfortable and enjoy connecting with audience members. For me the key is preparation – not just speech preparation but networking preparation. When I am prepared for networking, my anxiety drops. The more I network the easier it is to prepare and actively participate in networking.

During this chapter you will explore why and how to connect:

- before your speech, and

- after your speech.

Connecting before your speech

Connecting with your audience before you speak reduces anxiety about speaking in front of people you do not know. You are less likely to feel alone on stage when you have connected with your audience beforehand.

Aim to arrive at the venue early to complete your pre-speech set-up, before attendees arrive. Once attendees start to arrive, you want to be available to connect with them. Say hello and connect with as many attendees as time allows. Take a minute or two to get to know the people you are connecting with and not just say 'hi' and move on to the next person. Make a true connection, not just a fleeting one.

Recently I witnessed a speaker walking the room before the speech and was disappointed to see how little they cared about the opportunity to connect with their audience. Their attempt to connect included eye contact as they extended their hand for a handshake, they said "Hello, I'm (real name replaced with) Really Not Interested" as their eyes worked the room, and I said "I'm Kaylene" as they walked off. I definitely did not feel any connection with this speaker and from what I saw others did not either.

I believe it is more important to truly connect with attendees even if it means you cannot connect with everybody before the speech. When you are speaking to an attendee be in the moment with them. Give them your full attention. When I see a speaker truly connecting with some attendees before the speech, it sparks my curiosity and gets me excited as the speaker is demonstrating that they care about the audience. A speaker that cares about the audience is a speaker that I will connect with.

A benefit of connecting with the audience before your speech is that you may uncover a gem that you can weave into your speech – an example, an insight shared by one of the attendees, that will add value to the speech.

I am not a natural networker; I find confidence through planning how I will engage attendees before the speech. Before we look at planning, I want to share my speaking horror story as it highlights why I find planning important.

> As a 21-year-old, I was excited to be given the opportunity to speak at a homeless youth retreat. I arrived late on Friday afternoon, and I was scheduled to speak on the Sunday morning. I was nervous as this was my first paid speaking gig and my only experience as a speaker was in high school. I was told by the organiser, "Just tell them your story". I was to share my story of a young woman in the Australian Public Service who had recently purchased her first home. The aim was to give them hope that they too could have a career and achieve their goals.
>
> On the Friday evening, I met the attendees, and on the Saturday I spent all day with them. I felt comfortable and enjoyed getting to know them. They shared their stories with me and I shared mine. I was very comfortable with the attendees and extremely nervous about my speech. On the Sunday morning before I was to speak the organiser saw I was nervous and told me again, "Just tell them your story". I told my story, the same story I had shared throughout the weekend when talking with them. There was no new content, because I had openly shared my complete story with anyone who asked. The credibility I had built over the weekend was thrown out the window with my speech. I left them feeling underwhelmed by my story. I felt terrible and embarrassed.

Would my story have inspired them to believe they could achieve their goals if they had heard it for the first time on the Sunday morning? I like to think it would have.

I was unprepared to socially interact with attendees before my speech. When they asked who I was and what I did, I told them everything. This meant I had nothing new in my speech, and it was my greatest fail as a speaker.

When you speak to the attendees before your speech, don't do what I did. Learn from my speaking horror story. Give the attendees teasers about what is to come but never give away your full speech, your main points or overall message. You want them to experience it as intended when you deliver the speech.

I now plan for my pre-speech conversations. I think about my topic and come up with some questions to start the conversation. I practice asking open questions to allow the attendee to speak, and I listen.

Here are a sample of questions I have used:

- Where are you from?

- What do you do in the organisation?

- What brought you here tonight?

- What do you know about the topic?

- What are you looking for out of the topic today?

- What experience have you with the topic?

My preparation is not all about questions. I prepare my own introduction, a short and a longer version of my pitch. I can't assume that everyone will have read my bio before the event.

Short version: I'm Kaylene Ledgar. I'm on the program to speak about 'unlocking your story'. We all have stories within us, John, what is your story?

Long version: I'm Kaylene Ledgar, I am the author of 'Speaking, It's NOT Worse Than Death.' The fear of public speaking used to consume me. My aim is to erase the fear of public speaking and open the door to opportunities. I believe you don't need to fear speaking; speaking is a learned skill and you can master it. We all have unique stories to share, it is time to erase the fear and let the world hear our stories. What is your story?

I like to think about how I will wrap-up the conversation and continue connecting or get ready for presentation.

It has been wonderful speaking to you John. I hope you enjoy the presentation today. I look forward to hearing more as you unlock your story.

Conclude your pre-speech networking a few minutes before you are scheduled to speak. This will allow you time to prepare and relax before you are introduced.

Connecting after your speech

After your speech, there is an opportunity for you to sell your products or services and connect with the audience. Provide clear instructions to the audience during your conclusion. Let them know where to go and what to do.

If you are selling your products and services, I suggest you do this from a specific sales table. Set-up your sales table before your presentation begins. If you want it to remain hidden until the end of your presentation, then cover it with a table cloth. Engage the support of a helper to manage quick sales. This will allow you more time to focus on those that want to speak to you as well as make a purchase.

If you asked the audience to sign-up, say for a newsletter, make the process as easy as possible after the speech. Consider having a QR code or bit.ly link for the audience to sign-up themselves. If you want them to sign-up by filling in a form, I suggest you set this up on a table with pens and copies of the form along with a tray or box for completed forms. Enlist a support person to help you manage the sign-up process, as this will allow you to focus on connecting with attendees.

If you have no products or services to sell, I encourage you to remain after the presentation to connect with the audience. Even when you have had a question and answer, Q & A session, it's still good to provide the audience with the opportunity to connect with you. There may be some people in the audience who have a question but chose not to ask or lacked confidence to ask the question. If you make yourself available after the event, you provide a private opportunity for them to ask you their question. Manage your time with each of the attendees and if you find that one requires more of your time, you could offer to set-up a time to connect at a later date.

Be prepared with open questions related to the presentation:

- What is your take-away from the presentation?

- How will you apply what you have learnt today?

Speak to the event organiser about where best to set-up for post event sales, sign-up and conversation. You want to give the person you are connecting with your full attention. Therefore, I suggest you position yourself with your back to everybody else. This will help you maintain focus, even with everything else going on in the room.

Other strategies used by speakers and event organisers include:

- 'meet the speaker' session for VIP ticket holders
- 'have lunch with the speaker' for VIP ticket holders
- invite only bonus question and answer session, and
- master class for early bird attendees.

Providing these opportunities to connect with the speaker means the people attending these special sessions do not need to talk to you after the presentation and you can focus on other attendees.

Action: Prepare to connect before your speech.

Prepare and practice your pitch.

Prepare to connect before your speech by asking yourself the following:

- What open questions can I ask?
- How will I wrap-up a conversation?

Action: Prepare to connect after your speech.

Prepare to connect after your speech by asking yourself the following:

- What products or services will I offer the attendees?
- Who can help me with a sales table or sign-up table?

- How much time will I have to connect with the audience after the speech?

- What other strategies can I use to connect with the attendees after the speech?

Action: Develop your networking skills.

To develop your networking skills, attend networking events, visit community groups and practice connecting with people. The more you do it the more comfortable you will become with networking.

A final word on let's get social

Embrace the opportunity to connect with your audience before and after you speak. Always follow through on any promises you make.

A tip from Alicia, my friend and self-proclaimed Networking Rockstar – always be prepared to network and have your business card with you.

CHAPTER 11

Bringing It All together

> By the time you walk on that stage,
> you want to be Olympic ready.
> You do all the hard work leading up to the event and
> at the event you perform, just like an elite athlete.
> **PADDY KENNEDY, KENNEDY COMMUNICATION STUDIO**

The process and structure you have used to develop your speech was designed to help you internalise your message. As you bring it all together, your confidence will grow and your fear will shrink.

During this chapter you will:

- practice, practice, practice your speech
- give your speech a catchy title

- prepare your introduction
- centre yourself and your nerves, and
- gain tips for delivering your speech.

Practice, practice, practice

As my coach Paddy says, you want to be Olympic ready by time you walk on stage.

If you aren't Olympic ready, your fears may become a reality. When you are Olympic ready, you will be confident and your fear will be replaced with adrenaline as you are eager to deliver your speech.

To be Olympic ready you need to practice, practice and practice some more.

Practice your content, practice using any visual aids and practice the delivery.

To be Olympic ready follow these steps:

1. Record yourself reading your speech:

    - To bring energy to your reading of the speech, stand while your read. Use your full range of vocal variety in the reading.

    - This is your first test run, and will help you identify any words or phrases that you may stumble over.

    - Listen to the recording as it will help you to memorise the key words and phrases in your speech. I listen to mine in the car.

2. Practice without notes:

    - Begin practicing small sections of the speech one at a time. I use the speech structure map to break up the content to practice. I like to practice each section in order but it is not necessary when you are learning each section. Doing them out of order will work too.

    - As you become more confident with the delivery, start pulling it together. Practice the opening and first main point, then practice the first main point and second main point.

    - Finally, practice the full speech from start to finish.

    - Two of my favourite places to practice speech content are the car and in the pool walking.

3. Bring it all together and rehearse your speech:

    - Rehearse as you plan to deliver your speech, including visual aids, stage movement, facial and body movement and vocal variety.

    - If using a slide show, do at least one rehearsal without the slides because you want to be prepared if there is a technical problem on the day.

    - Rehearse in front of an audience. I have been known to rehearse in front of my cats, Dream and Magic, though human audiences work better as cats provide no feedback or encouragement.

    - Record your rehearsals and review them, noting any areas that you may need to focus on.

- Take note of the time it takes you to deliver your speech and make adjustments as required. If you have humour in your speech and expect laughter, allow extra time for live audience laughter. The bigger the audience the longer the laughter. I like to come in under time when I am rehearsing because when delivering the speech at the event, I might add in a line or give the audience more time to reflect or laugh. This allows me a buffer to still finish on time with any extras.

- The key is to rehearse, know your content and yet remain natural. You do not want to appear like a robot, even though you have scripted the speech.

How much practice is enough? It's a good question and one that only you can answer. The aim of the practice is to be confident that you have internalised the main points, your opening, your conclusion and you know your roadmap. My speeches when delivered are rarely word perfect to the script I prepared. While I will use majority of what I scripted, in the moment, I find other ways to express my point, and use different words and phrases. Remember only you know what you scripted therefore you can go off script in the moment and that is ok.

Remember to also practice your pre and post speech networking.

Give your speech a catchy title

Now is the time to give your speech a catchy title. This may be your overall message that you have used as your working title or a new title.

My working title for this book was 'You can overcome your fear of public speaking'. I brainstormed titles and my number one choice was 'It's NOT Worse Than Death, A speaker's guide for overcoming their fear of speaking'. In hindsight that title was too long and my trusted sources told me so. I listened to their feedback and refined the title to "Speaking, It's NOT Worse Than Death" – a much tighter, catchier title.

To find your speech title, I recommend that you brainstorm titles. Then select your top five speech titles and test them out by asking people for feedback.

- Which one do you like best and why?
- What comes to mind when you hear this title?

Use the feedback to refine and select the speech title. The speech title should be easy to remember and ideally ten words or less.

The speech title is your headline and you want it to be attractive to the listener. You want them to hear the title and spark their interest before you start speaking.

Prepare your introduction

I like to prepare a brief introduction to give to the person who will introduce me. The introduction will include my qualifications and experience, a teaser about the topic and my name. The purpose is to build your credibility before you speak and to get the audience excited about your topic.

> Having overcome her own fear of speaking Kaylene Ledgar is a certified World Class Speaking Coach who specialises in helping people overcome their fear of speaking. She is the author of 'Speaking, It's NOT Worse Than Death' and today she will be sharing her tips on how to bust your fear of speaking. Are you ready to bust your fear?
>
> With 'Bust Your Fear of Speaking', please welcome Kaylene Ledgar.

By taking control of your introduction you are setting your ideal scene for your introduction. By providing the introduction you reduce the risk of the person introducing you steeling your thunder by innocently sharing a key point from your speech.

If you can, I recommend emailing a copy of the introduction to the person introducing you at least a few days before the event.

Take a copy of the introduction with you on the day, just in case the person introducing you forgets to bring it.

Centre yourself and your nerves

Before I get out the car at the venue, I like to take a few moments to centre myself using visualisation and affirmation. Basically, I give myself a pep talk and ensure my mindset is focused on the event and the presentation.

Tips for managing any nerves before you go on stage:

1. Avoid alcohol before you speak.

2. Drink room temperature water. Cold water, especially icy cold water, can leave you breathless and you do not want that as you are going on stage.

3. Take a few moments for yourself before the start. Find a quiet place, away from the excitement in the room.

4. Listen to music. Select music that works for you. If you want to calm down, you may select a short relaxation or meditation piece. If you want to get the adrenaline pumping you might select your favourite song.

5. Take a few moments for a deep breathing exercise. Breathe in and out for the count of three. Be mindful not to make

yourself breathless. I suffer from asthma and at times this activity can make me more breathless. Know your body and your breath.

6. If your nerves are starting to surface, you may want to use a relaxation technique like tightening the toes, releasing the toes, tightening your fingers, releasing your fingers. Relax different parts of your body by first tensing then releasing.

I met a speaker years ago who would take their jacket and tie off then drop to the floor and do push-ups before competing in speech contests. The speaker was ex-military, thrived on competition and he found that doing push-ups released the tension of competition and helped him focus.

Find what works for you. For me I always turn to visualisation, affirmations, deep breathing and relaxation techniques. You may like the idea of dropping to the floor and doing push-ups or playing your favourite song. Find what works for you and do it.

Delivering your speech

You have rehearsed your delivery many times before today, now is the time to shine. Walk confidently to your starting point on the stage. Fix a natural smile on your face, unless you have another expression for the start of your speech. Make eye contact with the audience and deliver your opening lines.

As you move through your speech, your confidence will grow, because you have given this speech a number of times already. You have internalised the main points and overall message, and you know why you are giving this speech to this audience now.

Maintain eye contact with your audience for the duration of the speech, unless you deliberately don't make eye contact to make a point. Connect with all parts of the audience, front, middle, back, left, centre and right. If you find eye contact uncomfortable, look at peoples eyebrows or hairline. It will look like eye contact even though it is not. For major points and key phrases, hold eye contact with a person in the room before continuing to work the room. Avoid sweeping eye contact where there is no connection because you are constantly moving your eyes from one side of the room to the other.

Remember that pauses are your friend. Do not be afraid to briefly pause to gather your thoughts. If you do forget something, it's ok – remember you are the only one who knows your full script.

While you may be nervous, tell yourself you are enjoying this, and the audience is enjoying this. Shift your mindset and enjoy the moment. You are sharing yourself, gifting your knowledge, insight, story, so be proud and be in the moment.

Speaker day of event timeline

1. Arrive early for set-up including:

    - equipment set-up

    - sound testing

    - walking the stage, and

    - getting a feel for the stage from the audience's perspective.

2. Connect with attendees as they arrive.

3. Take a few moments to centre yourself before you are introduced.

4. Deliver your speech.

5. Connect with the attendees, sell products and services.

6. Pack-up equipment and leave venue.

Action: Practice, practice and practice some more.

Follow the steps to be Olympic ready:

1. Record yourself reading your speech.

2. Practice without notes.

3. Bring it all together and rehearse your speech.

Action: Give your speech a catchy title.

Use these 3 steps to select your speech title:

1. Brainstorm speech titles.

2. Select your top five speech titles and test them out by asking people for feedback.

    - Which one do you like best and why?

    - What comes to mind when you hear this title?

3. Use the feedback to refine and select the speech title.

Action: Prepare your introduction.

Write a brief introduction for your speech including:

- qualifications and experience
- a teaser about the topic, and
- your name.

If you can, email a copy to the person introducing you.

Take a copy of the introduction with you on the day.

Action: Manage any nerves before you go on stage.

Identify how you will manage your nerves before going on stage.

Action: Deliver your speech and connect with your audience.

Share your message with the audience and do your best to enjoy the moment.

A final word on bring it all together

Practice, practice and more practice.

You have done the hard work and are ready to delivery your presentation.

Good luck, remember to breathe and you will survive your speech.

CHAPTER 12

What Next?

Live to learn and you will really learn to live.
JOHN C. MAXWELL

Well done! You have delivered your first speech.

Now what? What do you do next?

You learn from it and you do it again!

The more you speak, the less you will fear speaking. Now that you have completed your first speech, you want to ensure that you learn from this experience, and maintain the skills you developed.

During this chapter you will:

- evaluate your speech
- continue your speaking skills development, and
- identify future speaking opportunities.

Evaluate your speech

The final part of all my speaking engagements is to complete an evaluation. I am always looking for opportunities to learn and to improve my content and my delivery. My evaluation includes:

- feedback from attendees and the event organiser, and
- reflection and completing my own self-evaluation.

If you plan on delivering the speech to a different audience, evaluating your speech will provide you with an opportunity to improve the presentation. There is always room for improvement.

If the speech you gave is one you will not repeat, like a eulogy, evaluating your speech will provide you with insight for when you prepare your next speech.

Feedback from attendees and the event organiser

Gathering feedback from attendees and the event organiser can be a formal or informal process. The formal process includes asking attendees to complete a 'speaker evaluation form', whereas the informal process is where I gather information from conversations with attendees and the event organiser.

When designing a 'speaker evaluation form', keep it short and simple. I like to include an opening comment to set the tone of why I am asking for feedback and a brief thank you at the end.

> As a speaker I am always looking to improve my presentation skills and content. I would greatly appreciate if you could take a few moments to provide me with feedback on today's presentation.
>
> Thank you for taking the time to provide feedback.

When designing the form, I avoid questions that rate the speaker on a scale. Using a scale is quick for the person filling in the form but I find it difficult to gain value from the ratings. I much prefer open questions that allow the speaker to write a few words that I can then work with. I like a mix of questions that highlight the strengths and value of the presentation along with questions that focus on improvements and inclusions.

Here are questions you can use to create a simple speaker evaluation form:

- What was most valuable to you in the presentation?

- What, if anything, was least valuable in the presentation?

- What, if anything, would you like to have been included in the presentation?

- What is your take-away from the presentation?

- What feedback, if anything, would you like to offer the presenter?

The risk when you use 'a speaker evaluation form' is sometimes people can be rude and nasty. Their comments are hurtful and simply add no value or opportunities for you to improve as a speaker or improve your content. If you come across an evaluation like this, read it, just in case there is some hidden value, then discard. If an attendee cannot respectfully provide you with feedback on how to improve, their feedback is not worth the time it takes to read it. Focus on the evaluations that provide you with valuable insight and opportunities to grow.

When seeking feedback from the organiser you can use a formal process, however I much prefer an informal process to review the objectives of the presentation and gather feedback on what worked and what could be improved. Use the information provided in the pre-event questionnaire to formulate questions to cover during the discussion. During the discussion, open the door for future speaking engagements by asking what other topics would be of value to your group.

I gain a lot from gathering feedback through conversations with attendees after the presentation. Asking targeted open questions and allowing the attendee to share their insights is valuable. While you are in the moment, you can ask additional questions and dig deeper than you can using an evaluation form.

Self-evaluation

While somewhat uncomfortable, watching a recording of your presentation is useful when doing a self-evaluation. I encourage you to start recording all of your presentations. Once you get over thoughts like "Oh my gosh, I look like that," "I didn't know I sounded like that," "Oh dear, look at me. What is all that nodding my head about?" "What am I doing with my hands?" "Why can't I stop touching my hair?" and "Do I really laugh at my own jokes that much?" you can gain great insight from observing yourself.

I find I am my harshest critic. I am always looking for opportunities to improve, therefore I always make time for reflection and self-evaluation after a presentation.

Here are some standard questions that I ask when completing my self-evaluation:

- What worked well?

- What moment or moments provided the greatest connection with the audience?

- Which, if any, parts of the speech felt awkward or uncomfortable?

- Which, if any, parts of the speech fell flat or below expectations?

- Did the humour hit the mark?

- Which parts, if any, created unexpected reactions from the audience?

- What, if anything, should I include next time?

- What, if anything, would I change or do differently?

- What did I learn about myself as a speaker?

Use your insights from the self-evaluation to enhance your speech or apply them to future speeches.

Continued learning

As a speaker, communicator and person, I believe there is always something to learn. As you have progressed through this book, you have been developing your speaking skills and knowledge. It is now time to revisit the self-assessment tool to see your improvements.

The self-assessment template can be used to further develop your skills and knowledge by following this process:

1. Complete the self-assessment template.

2. Select one area that you want to focus on for the next month. Identify what you can do to improve your skills and knowledge in this area.

3. At the end of the month, complete the self-assessment and see where you have improved.

4. Select another area to focus on for the next month.

When selecting an area to focus on, it is up to you where you want to start. Consider these questions:

- What interests me the most?

- What would bring me the most value?

There are many options available to improve your skills and knowledge:

- research the skill on the internet

- observe other speakers live or online

- read a book

- join a local or online Toastmasters Club

- sign-up for a workshop, and

- engage a coach.

If you focus on one of the 12 categories each month, in 12 months your skills, knowledge and your confidence will have grown considerably. Your fear of public speaking will be fading if not a distant memory.

Future speaking opportunities

By putting yourself out there and giving your speech, other speaking opportunities are likely to come your way. As a speaker you will gain credibility on your topic the more you share your message, and you will be seen as an expert, an influencer. I encourage you to embrace the opportunities as this will help you to continue to grow as a speaker and conquer any remaining fear you are holding on to.

Look for opportunities to speak and be the person that says "I will do it" when a speaker is needed. Look for opportunities at work, in the community and within your social network. Be the person at work who says, "yes, I will give the presentation". Be the person who says "yes, I will do the toast" at a family gathering. While others are shying away from the speaking opportunities, grab them with both hands. The more you do it the more confident you will be.

For me Toastmasters Clubs provide me with a safe and supportive environment to continue to develop my skills and to speak regularly. As a Toastmaster I embrace opportunities to speak in the club and outside the club at Toastmaster run events.

I found joining community and social committees opened the door for me to practice my speaking at meetings and when promoting the group to others.

Put the word out there that you have a story to share.

Action: Decide how you will gather feedback from attendees and the event organiser.

Will you use a 'speaker evaluation form' or will you use an informal method to gather feedback?

If using a speaker evaluation form, design your form.

Action: Complete self-assessment.

1. Complete the self-assessment template.

2. Compare your ratings and thoughts now to those when you completed the self-assessment template before you started creating your speech.

Speaker self-assessment template

Use this template to rate yourself on a scale of 1 to 10 for each skill. A score of 1 means you have no confidence or were unaware of this skill in speaking. A 10 means you are extremely confident and fully implement this skill in all your speeches.

In the thoughts column, note keywords and phrases that come to mind about your current skill level.

Skill	Rating	Thoughts
Busting your fear of public speaking How confident are you as a speaker?		

Skill	Rating	Thoughts
Getting started How confident are you about doing your speech homework?		
The right package How confident are you in defining the purpose and mapping the structure of your speech?		
Unlocking your story How confident are you with storytelling?		
To Q&A or not How confident are you with including a question and answer session in your speech?		
Bookends matter How confident are you with opening your speech to connect and creating a memorable conclusion?		
Using your voice How confident are you with using vocal variety in your speech?		

Skill	Rating	Thoughts
Making a move How confident are you with making purposeful movements during your speech?		
Selecting your accessories How confident are you with using props, slides and notes in your speech?		
Let's get social How confident are you networking with your audience before and after your speech?		
Bringing it all together How confident are you with practicing your speech?		
What next? How confident are you with evaluating your own speech and applying your learnings?		

Action: Continue to learn.

Focus on one of the 12 categories each month and in 12 months your skills, knowledge and confidence will have grown extensively.

1. Use the self-assessment template.

2. Select one area that you want to focus on for the next month.

3. Identify what you can do to improve your skills and knowledge in this area.

4. At the end of the month, complete the self-assessment and see where you have improved.

5. Select another area to focus on for the next month.

A final word on what's next

You have the momentum, you have developed your first speech, you want to keep going. The best advice I can give you is never stop learning to communicate. There is always something you can learn, there is always room for improvement, no matter how many times you have given a speech. I keep learning even with hundreds of speeches under my belt. Keep your speaking skills fresh and keep looking for opportunities to grow as a speaker. The key to conquering your fear of speaking is to continue to speak. Therefore, when asked what's next, say "I'm going to keep speaking".

Speaking It's NOT Worse Than Death

BONUS CHAPTER

From The Heart With Tears

According to most studies,
people's number 1 fear is public speaking.
Number 2 is death. Death is number 2!
This means, to the average person, if you go to a funeral,
you're better off in the casket than doing the eulogy.
JERRY SEINFELD

◆ ◆ ◆

The most difficult, yet most important speeches of my life have been the tributes for those that have passed.

I was first asked to give my grandparents' eulogies following a two-minute toast that I presented at my grandad's 80th birthday party. As soon as I had finished, my grandma turned to me and said, "You can do my eulogy." Quickly followed by Grandad, "You can do mine too." I was surprised and honoured at the same time. Both were in good health and the thought of funerals were far from my mind. Looking at them, loving them, how could I refuse? I agreed to do their eulogies.

When I told Darling, my dad's mum, about this, she liked the idea and asked me to do her eulogy too. Since then, I have delivered the eulogy for Grandad and Darling. I delivered a eulogy at a friend's funeral and helped another friend prepare a eulogy for a mutual friend. When my dad was diagnosed with stage 4 cancer late 2018, he didn't ask me to give his eulogy, he just knew I would. In Dad's final weeks, I was asked if I thought I would be ok to deliver the eulogy and I simply said, "I have to, he is my dad, I will do it for him and I will do it for the family." Early 2019, 13 weeks after Dad was diagnosed, I stood in front of my family and friends, grieving the greatest loss of my life, as I delivered the speech of my life, my dad's eulogy.

In times of grief, if I can make it easier for the family and for the friends, I will stand up and I will do the eulogy. Honouring the life of a loved one is difficult, however, when faced with grief, the fear of speaking is less painful than the loss. Standing up while consumed with grief and speaking is not easy, whether you are doing it for the first time or you have done it before.

Delivering a eulogy is difficult even when you are a confident speaker. If you fear speaking, your automatic response when asked to deliver a eulogy is likely to be "no". You may find yourself saying:

Why would I want to put myself in that position?

Why do something I fear?

What if I make a mistake?

I'm grieving, I just can't do it.

From my experience, when we shift our focus from "I" and focus on the family, you just have to say "yes" when asked. The family asked you to give the eulogy for a reason, they could have asked another but they chose you. They believe you are the right person for this important role. Trust their judgement that you are the right person for this special job.

When you deliver a eulogy, you speak from your heart, you respectfully honour the person and provide comfort to the family and mourners. With the focus on the person you are honouring and their loved ones, you shift the focus away from you, and you can rise above your fear.

In most cases there is only a few days from when you are asked to give a eulogy and when you deliver it. This bonus chapter is designed to help you pull together a eulogy, with confidence, in a few days.

The process I share to help you with preparing and delivering a eulogy can be adapted for other celebration speeches.

During this chapter you will unlock the three doors that help me speak from the heart with tears:

- getting started
- the right package, and
- bringing it all together.

Getting started

You have said "yes", you will deliver the eulogy, but where do you start?

Like with any speech, you want to do your homework before you start creating the speech. The getting started door is where you unlock information about the service, clarify expectations of family and identify key information about the person you will be honouring.

Information about the service

To help you prepare for the eulogy you will want to know details about the service including:

- When and where will the service be held?
- How long is allocated for the eulogy?
- Who will be leading the service?
- Will there be other speakers or tributes?

At the time of being asked to deliver the eulogy, some of the details about the service may not be available. Without this information you can continue preparing.

The time allocated for the eulogy varies. I have had from as little as five minutes to as long as 18 minutes. If the timing is unknown when you start preparing your speech, I would focus on preparing a five-minute eulogy. It is easier to add more content if you are allowed more time.

Clarifying the expectations of family

While the eulogy is about the person being honoured, it is important to clarify expectations with the family. They, as you are, will be grieving. Grief takes on many forms and we all grieve differently. Early days of grief are often filled with shock and sadness, so it can be difficult for family members to know what they want from the eulogy. This is where you may need to guide them by asking a few questions:

- Is there anything you do not want me to include in the eulogy?

- Is there anything you specifically want me to include?

- I will come up with a plan for the eulogy, would you like me to share that with you before I start writing the eulogy?

- Are their people that you would like me to talk to who might have stories or insights that I might be able to use in the eulogy?

- Is there anyone you would like me to acknowledge or thank when I deliver the eulogy?

Identify key information

To uncover key information about the person being honoured spend time with family members and friends. Listen to their stories and make notes. Capture details, keywords and phrases. Share your memories and stories with the family and add them to your notes.

You want to gather information that will help define the character, the heart of the person. What made this person unique? What made people love them? You want to capture stories and insights that will remind those grieving of the wonderful life their loved one lived.

The eulogy is about the person, not about you and not just about your relationship with them. That said, I feel it is important that you do share what they meant to you and your own personal insights.

Here is a guide of the type of information you can gather:

- When and where were they born?

- Did they have any nicknames?

- Early years
    - Who were their parents?
    - Did they have any siblings?
    - Where did they go to school?
    - Did they have any significant education or other achievements while at school?
    - What were their interests as a child and teenager?
    - What did they want to be or do when they grew up?
- Family
    - Did they have a partner? If yes, who are they and when did they meet?
    - Did they have children, grandchildren/great grandchildren? If yes, who are they?
    - What are some of the beautiful memories about their time together?
    - What is something the loved ones will miss about the person?
- Career, business
    - What did they do for a living?
    - Who did they work for?
    - What was their role?
    - Did they have any significant career achievements?

- Hobbies and interests
    - Were they a member of any clubs?
    - Did they have a favourite sports team?
    - What did they enjoy doing?
    - How did they spend most of their time?
    - What was their favourite pastime?

In their words

To be able to speak the words of the person you are honouring provides a special moment for all.

If you know in advance that you will be asked to deliver a eulogy, you can gather information directly. Encourage them to talk and share their stories, ask them questions and take notes. If you can, ask them to sum up their life.

When I asked my dad about his life, his message was clear: "I have no regrets." Dad, knowing his time was limited, was very clear on what he wanted me to share with people. He wanted to specifically thank people for their contribution to his amazing life. I shared his words, his thank you at the service, I spoke his words when he no longer could.

You may want to start a journal, capturing special moments in your life and the lives of those you love. You never know when you may be called upon to speak and having a journal of stories will make it easier for you to prepare the speech or eulogy.

Right package

Having gathered key information and listened to many stories, you then need to decide what will be included in the eulogy. It is likely that you have enough stories to fill a book, which means you will need to carefully select what you can realistically cover in the eulogy.

The first part of the right package door is turning key points into a structure, and the second part is writing the eulogy in full.

Turning key points into a structure

Firstly, review all of your notes and identify 3 to 5 key themes – this will be body of your eulogy. The key themes may be early years, family, career and interests.

In addition to the body of the eulogy, you will have an opening and a conclusion.

The opening is where you can introduce yourself if the person leading the service has not introduced you and your relationship to the person being honoured. In the opening, you will introduce the person you are honouring.

The conclusion is where you share the person's own words. Your final words should highlight the essence of the person and the mark they have left on this world.

You may also want to include a thank you for people who have travelled a distanced to be there or to medical staff or others. In my dad's eulogy I acknowledged the oncologists and nursing staff at the hospital. I also acknowledged the support of my dad's sister-in-law, my aunt Sharen, who worked at the hospital and was there every step of the way looking after Dad and the family. Let the family guide who you should acknowledge and thank. You do not want to be thanking by name a lot of people – thank key people by name only, then offer a more general thank you.

If you are not a family member, you may want to offer your condolences to the family before your final words.

Here is a sample outline for a eulogy:

- Opening, introduce yourself and the person you are honouring.

- Early years, parents, siblings, schooling.

- Family, their partner, children, grandchildren.

- Career, what they did for a living.

- Interests, sports, activities they were into.

- Thank you to key people.

- Conclusion, condolences to the family, a final word about the person and the mark they have left.

Using the sample outline with five minutes allocated for the eulogy, you will have approximately 50 seconds for each of the key themes and 50 seconds for the opening and conclusion combined. You may decide that you want to allocate more time to one key theme over another. That is fine, there is no rule that says you have to allocate each key theme the same amount of time. You may choose to allocate more time to interests, taking it to 90 seconds, and less time to career and thank you, dropping them to 30 seconds each.

I speak on average 135 words per minute, so for a for a five-minute speech that is approximately 675 words. If you want to you can work out your average words per minute – time yourself as you read out loud. Divide the total words read by the time it took, and this will give you your average words per minute.

Writing the eulogy

Now that you have your outline, it is time to start writing the eulogy. Finding the right words can be hard. I recommend that when you begin try to write and not think about the actual words. You can review and edit when you have the initial draft captured.

Sometimes it is easier to speak out the eulogy using voice to text software. If you choose to do this, use the structure that you prepared as a guide and simply talk out each of the parts. As with when you write out the eulogy, don't worry about saying the right words, just capture your words, then review and edit later.

Don't think that you have to find all the words for the eulogy yourself. You spent time with the family and friends, you listened to their stories, they gave you the words and you can use them. I feel by using the words of others in the eulogy, it provides a small comfort to them. It makes the moment extra special for them as they know their special moment is being shared.

Stories are powerful, they evoke memories and help drive home key points. A simple technique to illustrate your key themes in the eulogy is to tell a story, then make a point. I have also done the reverse for eulogies, making the point then sharing a story.

In the time allocated, you can't share everything, therefore selecting stories that will demonstrate the point is better than providing a shopping list of attributes and achievements.

Once you have written or spoken the draft eulogy, take a break, grab a cuppa, go for a walk, clear your mind, then come back with a clear head to review and edit. As you review, look for opportunities to tighten the content without losing the message. If you find that in the draft you are using an adjective repeatedly, you may want to use the thesaurus function to find a different word.

As you practice the eulogy, you can continue to make changes. I have been known to make changes right up till the moment I stand to deliver the eulogy.

Bringing it all together

As you bring it all together, make sure you take care of yourself and work through your own feelings of grief.

Practice reading the eulogy out loud

Due to the short time frame, you will want to jump right in and start practicing as you plan to deliver the eulogy. That means practice with your notes the way they will be printed on the day.

Here are my tips for using notes:

- Use large font. The font should be easily read from a standing position if you drop the page on the floor. I used to recommend Arial 22 point however as my eyes are getting old, this does not work for me. Find the font size that works best for you.

- Use double spacing or 1 ½ spacing. This will give you room to make changes in pen and makes it easier to see the words.

- Start each sentence on a new line.

- Add an extra line between paragraphs. This will help you pause, breathe and continue while filled with emotions.

- Number each of the pages.

- Print single sided.

- Place all pages on the right-hand side of the lectern.

- As you near the end of the page, slowly move the page to the left. Doing this will allow you to move to the top of the next page easily.

- As you read your speech, lift your eyes regularly to make contact with the audience.

- Use your finger as a guide – this will help you easily find your place when your eyes return to the script.

- Practice reading the speech and lifting your eyes. If you can do it in front of a mirror, do so, as this way you can lift your eyes, make eye contact with yourself, before looking back at the script. The more you practice the easier it will be to read the script and make eye contact with the audience.

If you are worried about your nerves or emotions getting the better of you, consider putting a prompt on each page top right-hand corner to help you maintain focus. To help me stay focussed I would consider using a red heart, a symbol of love or a sunflower, a symbol to stand tall and proud or a smiley face, a symbol to prompt me to smile.

As you practice, make any necessary changes. If you find you are stumbling over a word, consider changing it. If you find particular words hard to deliver, is there another way you can phrase it that is easier to say? For me, when I delivered my dad's eulogy, I referred to him mostly as David because referring to him as Dad simply hurt too much and I knew I would struggle to hold it together. Using David throughout the eulogy meant that when I was sharing my own words, the words from my heart, I could say Dad and while it hurt, I managed. Sharing stories from others helped, because I could focus on the person whose story I was sharing and it gave me strength.

Time yourself reading the eulogy out loud a few times to ensure that you will be within the allocated time. If you are consistently taking longer than allocated to read the eulogy, consider where you can remove or tighten up some content. A story that is four or more sentences may need to be shortened to two or three sentences.

Delivering the eulogy

On the day, make sure you pack your notes, water at room temperature - not icy cold - and a small packet of tissues. If you can, arrive early and introduce yourself to the person leading the service. Confirm how and when you will be introduced. Take a moment to gather yourself. It can be quite confronting walking in and seeing the coffin or photos for the first time. Familiarise yourself with the area where you will be speaking from. Stand behind the lectern and look at the room. Secure a seat that will allow you to easily make your way to the lectern. Take a few moments for yourself before speaking to family and other guests.

Take your seat along with the other mourners. As it nears the time for you to deliver the eulogy, it may help to do a deep breathing exercise where you breathe in for the count of three, hold for the count of three and exhale to the count of three. Taking a small sip of water can help calm the nerves. Remember as you stand to walk to the lectern, the family asked you to do this, they believe in you, you are doing this for the person you are honouring and their family. You have practiced and you are ready.

While delivering the eulogy, you may have tears – let them flow. If the emotion starts to impact on your voice or you feel that you are about to break, pause and take a deep breath before continuing. You are allowed to take that moment to gather yourself before you move on – this will also give the attendees a moment to gather themselves before you continue. If the deep breathing didn't do the trick, taking a sip of water can be enough to break that emotion. If you used a symbol on your notes, focus on the symbol while you pause. Once you are ready continue with the eulogy.

After the service has concluded, be prepared for people to approach you. If you need a moment to gather yourself, find a quiet place. From my experience, people will want to thank you for your words, comment about something that was said or share their own story. It can be quite overwhelming and I find taking a few moments for yourself is necessary.

Action: Complete the getting started template.

Information about the service

When and where will the service be held?

How long is allocated for the eulogy?

Who will be leading the service?

Will there be other speakers or tributes?

Expectations of the family

Is there anything you do not want me to include in the eulogy?

Is there anything you specifically want me to include?

I will come up with a plan for the eulogy, would you like me to share that with you before I start writing the eulogy?

Are their people that you would like me to talk to who might have stories or insights that I might be able to use in the eulogy?

Is there anyone you would like me to acknowledge or thank when I deliver the eulogy?

Identifying key information

When and where were they born?

Did they have any nicknames?

Early years

> Who were their parents?
>
> Did they have any siblings?
>
> Where did they go to school?
>
> Did they have any significant education or other achievements while at school?
>
> What were their interests as a child and teenager?
>
> What did they want to be or do when they grew up?

Family

> Did they have a partner? If yes, who are they and when did they meet?
>
> Did they have children, grandchildren/great grandchildren? If yes, who are they?
>
> What are some of the beautiful memories about their time together?
>
> What is something the loved ones will miss about the person?

Career, business

> What did they do for a living?

Who did they work for?

What was their role?

Did they have any significant career achievements?

Hobbies and interests

Were they a member of any clubs?

Did they have a favourite sports team?

What did they enjoy doing?

How did they spend most of their time?

What was their favourite pastime?

Action: Create the right package.

Select the key themes for the eulogy and create an outline for the eulogy.

Opening:

Key theme 1:

Key theme 2:

Key theme 3:

Thank you:

Conclusion:

Using the outline write the eulogy. You may elect to speak out the eulogy using voice to text software.

Review and edit the draft eulogy.

Action: Bring it all together.

Practice the eulogy, using your notes.

Deliver the eulogy.

A final word on from the heart with tears

You have been given an opportunity that most people would refuse. By following this simple process, you will be able to honour your loved one while providing comfort to their family and friends. It takes a special person to say "yes" and when you take a moment to reflect on what you have done; appreciate the gift you have given and be proud.

Speaking It's NOT Worse Than Death

Afterword

Stay strong and live your life with no regrets.
DAVID LEDGAR

Congratulations!

You have unlocked the vital keys to busting your fear of public speaking and have shut the door on your fear.

To keep the door shut, continue to learn, continue to practice and keep speaking. If you drop your momentum the door to your fear will creep open.

Over the years, I have noticed that speakers who speak more frequently become stronger speakers and build their confidence quicker. Speakers who speak less often take longer to develop their skills and struggle to conquer their fear. When you do not speak frequently, the door to your fear remains ajar and your fear is present. The best way to close the door firmly is to speak regularly.

It's like riding a bike. As a child you learn to ride a bike, then you stop riding the bike for a number of years. As an adult you decide to get back on the bike and while you know how to pedal and steer the bike, you are not as confident and might be a bit wobbly – or maybe very wobbly. You may even find yourself falling off the bike or crashing the bike. With regular practice, you regain your confidence and ability to ride safely.

Throughout this book you have learnt the keys to creating a powerful speech; you don't want to lose them. Keep them front of mind as your prepare your future speeches. Look for opportunities to speak and to share your story. When you do not have speaking engagements, share your stories with family, friends and people you meet. Become a masterful storyteller on and off the stage.

If you are ready to accelerate your speaking skills or would like more support overcoming your fear, you can contact me by visiting my website, www.kayleneledgar.com.au.

Continue to speak and keep the door to your fear firmly closed.

Having busted your fear of speaking, keep unlocking your stories and let the world hear your voice.

To your speaking success,

About the Author

Kaylene Ledgar is on a mission to erase the fear of speaking. Kaylene says "You don't need to fear speaking; speaking is a learned skill and you can master it."

16 years ago, Kaylene made the life-changing decision to face her fear of speaking. Fear of speaking used to consume her, but now with hundreds of speaking opportunities under her belt, she is a motivational speaker who helps others to overcome their fear of speaking.

Kaylene believes that when our actions match our values, we unlock our true path. In 2019, she decided to close the door on her 26 year career in the Australian Public Service to be a full-time coach, speaker and live her true path.

Kaylene is a certified World Class Speaking Coach. She has a Diploma of Government - Management and Certificate IV Training and Assessment. She has been a member of Toastmasters International for 16 years, regularly volunteering for leadership roles at Club and District levels.

Kaylene is the eldest child of David and Lavinia, sister to John and David, and mother to her two cats, Dream and Magic. After 16 years living interstate, Kaylene has recently returned home to Frankston South, Victoria, Australia.

Kaylene can be contacted through her website:

www.kayleneledgar.com.au

Speaking It's NOT Worse Than Death

Acknowledgements

*Investing in the right support, at the right time,
put me on the right path.*
KAYLENE LEDGAR

I have been on an extraordinary journey from first overcoming my fear of public speaking and developing my skills as a speaker, to training to be a speaker coach and taking the plunge to set-up my own business, and finally pulling it all together to publish this book.

Mine was not a solo journey, and as I realise my dream, I want to acknowledge those that were part of my journey.

Overcoming my fear of speaking started with Toastmasters International, a non-profit educational organisation that teaches public speaking and leadership skills through a worldwide network of clubs. Joining Tuggeranong Toastmasters Club in 2003, I never would have imagined that speaking would become my passion and helping others overcome their fear my purpose. To all the Toastmasters near and far who have been part of my journey, thank you for helping me unlock my fear and develop my skills as a speaker. If you are looking for a safe environment to develop and practice your speaking, I recommend you visit a local or online Toastmasters Club.

When it came time to marry my passion for speaking with my desire to help people speak, I was drawn to the World Class Speaking Coach certification program. The program was designed and run by Craig Valentine, 1999 World Champion of Public Speaking and Mitch Meyerson, Founder of Guerrilla Marketing Coaching. Throughout the program I learnt what it takes to be a World Class Speaker, how to be a World Class Speaking Coach and how to establish my own coaching business. Becoming a certified World Class Speaking Coach opened the door for a career change, an opportunity to realise my dream. If you have a passion for speaking and coaching, I highly recommend the World Class Speaking Coach certification program, and learn all you can from Craig and Mitch.

For years, I privately dreamt of being a published author but didn't know where to start or what I would write. Then I met the sensational Natasa Denman and was introduced to the Ultimate 48-hour Author. In her half day Blueprint for Ultimate Book Writing Success Workshop, Natasa revealed her successful system for getting your book written in just 48 hours. I signed-up for the Ultimate 48-hour Writers Retreat, followed the program set-out by Natasa and now I'm writing the acknowledgement in my book. In my wildest dreams, I never expected to be saying "my book". Natasa and the Ultimate 48-hour Author crew of Stuart Denman and Vivienne Mason nurture and guide new authors from a seed of an idea, to publishing your book and beyond. If writing a book is a dream of yours, make it a reality with Ultimate 48-hour Author.

Finally, I am living my dream because of the talented speakers that I have mentored and coached over the years. They challenge me, excite me and motivate me to keep following my dream.

FREE Resources

Visit www.kayleneledgar.com.au/speechprepwb to download your FREE copy of:

- Speaking, It's NOT Worse Than Death workbook. You can use this to prepare your future speeches.

Visit www.kayleneledgar.com.au/eulogywb to download your FREE copy of:

- From the Heart with Tears workbook for preparing a eulogy. You can use this to prepare any celebration style speech.

Kaylene Ledgar
COACH

Kaylene believes "You don't need to fear speaking; speaking is a learned skill and you can master it."

Having struggled with a fear of talking to a group of two or more, Kaylene was able to build her confidence and find her own authentic voice. Her transformation is attributed to her passion for learning and challenging herself to face her own fear.

Kaylene is now a coach, speaker and author. By uniting her passion with her values, Kaylene has unlocked her true path.

As a coach, Kaylene works with new and experienced speakers, building their confidence and skills as a speaker.

*Kaylene is a thoroughly knowledgeable, yet humble, educator with a wealth of experience which she willingly imparts to fledgling public speakers. She has the incredible and rare skill of empathising with every speaker at whatever stage of their development. Kaylene is then able to provide compelling and challenging feedback to enable them to boldly take their next steps towards achieving their dreams. ~ **Arnjali Amarasingham, Senior Government Lawyer, Department of Human Services***

*I was fortunate enough to have Kaylene coaching me over a period of time, during which she tailored her approach to my needs and focusing areas. The coaching sessions she provided me were comprehensive, educational and motivational, and filled with lots of timely constructive feedbacks and I could feel almost immediate improvement on my speech construction and delivery. The tips, suggestions, exercises and feedback that she offered me are useful and effective, and I can see positive results derived since then on my personal skills, social interactions and career development. You learn, improve, and get inspired and enlightened from Kaylene on this value-adding development journey. ~ **Queenie Wei, Financial Analyst, Treasury***

COACHING PACKAGES

Kaylene offers Coaching Packages by application only. During the chat you will explore your speaking goals and the next steps, while uncovering if you and Kaylene are a match. Packages and pricing structures are discussed over a 20-minute qualifying conversation.

To schedule your qualifying conversation, visit www.kayleneledgar.com.au/coaching and submit an enquiry for qualifying conversation.

Kaylene Ledgar
SPEAKER

Kaylene believes "You don't need to fear speaking; speaking is a learned skill and you can master it."

Having struggled with a fear of talking to a group of two or more, Kaylene was able to build her confidence and find her own authentic voice. Her transformation is attributed to her passion for learning and challenging herself to face her own fear.

Kaylene is now a coach, speaker and author. By uniting her passion with her values, Kaylene has unlocked her true path.

An inspirational speaker who will entertain, educate and empower you to face your fear of speaking and unleash the speaker within.

Kaylene's presents her signature topics as keynotes and workshops:

BUST YOUR FEAR OF SPEAKING

- Face your fear
- Speaking without fear
- Speaking is a learned skill

UNLOCK YOUR STORY TREASURER CHEST

- Find your story
- 6Cs of storytelling
- Bring your story to life

CRYSTAL CLEAR SPEECHES

- Uncover your message
- The right package
- 3Ps of speaking

"Professional, eloquent and articulate, Kaylene is a top speaker and presenter, who enthralls audiences with her style. Kaylene's coaching style is transformational and I would recommend her to all who want to become the best version of themselves." ~ David A Hughes, Speaker and Facilitator, I Can Do Words

To engage Kaylene to speak at your event, visit www.kayleneledgar.com.au/speaking and submit an enquiry.

www.ingramcontent.com/pod-product-compliance
Lightning Source LLC
Chambersburg PA
CBHW031110080526
44587CB00011B/908